A Brief Guide to Business Classics

From *The Art of War* to *The Wisdom of Failure*

James M. Russell

ROBINSON

ROBINSON

First published in Great Britain in 2017 by Robinson

A CIP catalogue record for this book
is available from the British Library

ISBN: 978-1-47213-960-3

Typeset in Garamond by SX Composing DTP, Rayleigh, Essex
Printed and bound in Great Britain by CPI Group (UK) Ltd, Croydon CR0 4YY

Papers used by Robinson are from well-managed forests
and other responsible sources

Robinson
An imprint of
Little, Brown Book Group
Carmelite House
50 Victoria Embankment
London EC4Y 0DZ

An Hachette UK Company
www.hachette.co.uk

www.littlebrown.co.uk

James M. Russell has a philosophy degree from the University of Cambridge, a post-graduate qualification in critical theory, and has taught at the Open University in the UK. He is the author of *A Brief Guide to Philosophical Classics* (Robinson, 2015) and *A Brief Guide to Spiritual Classics* (Robinson, 2016). He lives in north London with his wife, daughter and two cats.

Also by James M. Russell:

A Brief Guide to Spiritual Classics
A Brief Guide to Philosophical Classics

Contents

Introduction

The world of business books is a curious place. Here you can find everything from great business people like Warren Buffett, Steve Jobs and Elon Musk, to the most spectacular business failures such as Enron and the subprime business market. You can find geniuses, hard workers, academics and entrepreneurs as well a few charlatans and hucksters. There's even room for Donald Trump. All human life is here, basically.

So how to choose which seventy titles to include in a collection of business classics? We had a few parameters in mind. Firstly, we wanted to include titles that dealt with a full range of areas of business, from sales and marketing to negotiation, entrepreneurship to investing, leadership to innovation, and from traditional and corporate models of business to start-up manuals and alternative angles on the subject.

There are some obvious best-selling titles such as *How to Make Friends and Influence People* or *7 Habits of Highly Effective People* that we felt we had to include. At the same time there are titles that are of more questionable value but that are often recommended on lists of business classics – for these we felt we should include a good range if only to warn readers away from the most egregious or flawed examples.

We also wanted to cover a wide span of time and to acknowledge that some of the most powerful or entertaining insights into business can be found in texts that aren't perceived as being 'business books'; for instance, *The Art of War*, *Microserfs*, *Thinking Fast and Slow* and *The Wealth of Nations*. And we aimed to bring the story of business titles up to date through the twentieth and early twenty-first centuries. We particularly wanted to include a good range of the most recent successes in business publishing as these are titles that readers may as yet be less familiar with. It seemed that the best way to organise such a disparate group of titles was to place them in chronological order, as this allows the reader to dip in and also casts an interesting light on how trends in business titles have changed over the years.

Among these titles, you will find expert advice, based on solid research (for instance, *The Effective Executive* or *Getting to Yes*), and inspirational guides to setting up businesses and running them on sound foundations (such as *True North*, *Crucial Conversations* or *We)*, alongside dubious management manuals that take a single flawed idea and stretch it out to the point of absurdity (let's be kind and not name the worst culprits yet).

Each book is summarised to convey a brief idea of what each one has to offer the interested reader, while a Speed Read of each book delivers a quick (occasionally flippant) sense of what each writer is like to read and a highly compressed summary of the main points of the book in question. The hope is that the reader will be inspired to read the best of these titles, ignore the worst of them and will come away with at least a basic idea of what each has to teach us about business.

James M. Russell

The Art of War

Sun Tzu, c. 500 BCE

The Art of War is a classic Chinese text from about 500 BCE. Its authorship is disputed, but it is generally credited to the military philosopher Sun Tzu, who would have been writing in the period when the various Chinese fiefdoms started to come together into a single enduring empire.

It has long been regarded as a military classic, but because it deals with situations of conflict, it has also been used as a key text in other contexts, including sport, the law and business negotiation. It was traditionally required reading for all executives at Japanese corporations and, from the 1980s onwards, acquired a cachet among Western business people, having been extensively quoted in the movie *Wall Street* by Gordon Gekko, a character who embodied the worst excesses of acquisitive, aggressive capitalism.

The slightly dubious reputation this gave the book was undeserved, and its popularity has persisted in business circles to this day. Sun Tzu is no mindless aggressor: he comes from the Taoist tradition and large parts of the book are devoted to avoiding conflict rather than seeking or initiating it. His basic assumption is that conflict is inevitable in (and between) human societies, but that warfare is a last resort, and one that will generally be damaging to all sides – one well-known quote is that 'the greatest victory is that which requires no battle'. The book proceeds on the basis that when faced with conflict you will often be able to avoid warfare, but need to be prepared to win when it can't be avoided.

Some modern readers find it hard to get past the idea of business as warfare, but if you can accept this book as a source of advice for dealing with conflicts of all sorts, it can be as useful as any more recent source. The book is divided into thirteen short chapters which deal with everything from initial assessment of your situation, planning and preparation, and how to win loyalty in your troops, through to making and deploying military strategies and adapting them as circumstances and the terrain changes.

At the broadest level Sun Tzu's advice is about keeping the initiative at all times: he writes that 'all warfare is based on deception. Hence, when we are able to attack, we must seem unable; when using our forces, we must appear inactive; when we are near, we must make the enemy believe we are far away; when far away, we must make him believe we are near.'

Similarly, he devotes much time to advising you to assess your opponents' capabilities with care, even down to such details as noting whether they have used up their food resources by slaughtering the last cattle (because this would indicate an enemy who is prepared to fight to the death). A large part of the text is premised on the idea that you may not be stronger than your opponent – indeed you may be the weaker party. However, by appearing 'weak when you are strong and strong when you are weak', you can nonetheless find strategic advantages even in the most unpromising of circumstances. And this will include knowing when not to fight and when to leave your opponents an escape route so that you don't force them to fight to the death if you can't guarantee to win that fight easily.

Sun Tzu also focuses on the costs of war. Prolonged warfare will benefit neither side so he advises resorting to warfare only where you can get a decisive result in a short period of time. There are obvious lessons here for modern businesses as they consider new initiatives and directions as well as the costs and opportunities to be gained from taking on their competitors in price wars or launching competing products.

Even some of his most specific advice can yield interesting morals. For instance, he talks about the usefulness of spies in very matter-of-fact terms, advising that you should use them because your opponents will certainly be doing so. And he suggests that, rather than carry food to battle, you steal food from your opponents, thus weakening them while saving your own energies in the journey. While it is hard to see an exact parallel for this in business practice, one could make comparisons with the costs and benefits of training up your own staff as opposed to recruiting or headhunting staff who already have the necessary skills.

How much you enjoy *The Art of War* may ultimately depend on how much you like reading about warfare and military strategy. But even for those who don't, this is a book that can glean interesting insights in dispute resolution and the avoidance of damaging conflicts, and the importance of knowing your enemy (or competitors) well.

The Art of War

There are five essentials for victory:

1. He will win who knows when to fight and when not to fight.
2. He will win who knows how to handle both superior and inferior forces.
3. He will win whose army is animated by the same spirit throughout all its ranks.
4. He will win who, prepared himself, waits to take the enemy unprepared.
5. He will win who has military capacity and is not interfered with by the sovereign.

The *I Ching*

Traditional

The *I Ching* is an ancient Chinese text that gradually took shape over the tenth to fourth centuries BCE. Its original use was almost certainly as a book of divination and that is how it is often described today. But in Taoist and Confucian culture it is just as likely to be used as a guide to moral decision-making.

It might seem like a peculiar choice of book to describe as a business classic. It is essentially a collection of short texts, from which you select a reading on any given occasion by generating a random series of numbers. (Traditionally this was done by throwing yarrow stalks, but most modern texts will also explain how to do so using coins or dice.) You can then be directed to any one of sixty-four 'hexagrams', each of which gives a poetic overview of a subject such as 'conflict', 'enthusiasm' or 'innocence', along with some interpretative text and individual lines that elaborate on the main text. The advice in the book often seems archaic or obscure and is aimed at ancient rulers dealing with issues of famine and plenty, war and peace.

However, if used in the right spirit, the *I Ching* can be surprisingly revealing. You first need to think of a question. And it is surprising how often in life we forget to ask the right questions. In business, for instance, it is extremely easy to get bogged down in generating this quarter's projections and last year's sales reports and in trying to work out how to meet current targets, while forgetting to foster the medium-to-long-term goals that will in the end be far more crucial for the individual and for the company. So to be forced to take a step back and consider what questions you need to ask is a good start towards thinking more reflectively about your job or business.

The second reason the *I Ching* can be useful is that it can tell us a lot about what we genuinely feel. Imagine that I ask the question, 'What should I do to grow my business over the next three years?' and randomly generate the hexagram 'waiting' in response. There I will read an admonition to patience, including the following lines:

> The rain will come in its own time. We cannot make it come; we have to wait for it. The idea of waiting is further suggested by the attributes of the two trigrams – strength within, danger in front. Strength in the face of danger does not plunge ahead but bides its time, whereas weakness in the face of danger grows agitated and has not the patience to wait . . . a strong man can stand up to his fate, for his inner security enables him to endure to the end. This strength shows itself in uncompromising truthfulness [with himself]. It is only when we have the courage to face things exactly as they are, without any sort of self-deception or illusion, that a light will develop out of events, by which the path to success may be recognised.

Now, this is quite powerful advice in its own right. But the important thing is how I respond to it: it might be that the text has some genuine relevance to my situation and that it makes me realise my own impatience in the face of obstacles. On the other hand, I may react with irritation, feeling that this is actually a moment when the right path is to press ahead without fear. Either way, by choosing a random text, I have been forced to contemplate what my true feelings are with respect to the question I asked.

Obviously, this wouldn't work with a text generated completely at random. But the point about the *I Ching* is that it contains many wise words about personal conduct, leadership, fate and respect. For example, the hexagram on 'youthful folly' contains pertinent advice on recognising one's limitations and looking to learn from those with more experience. While the text below from the 'holding together' hexagram is powerful advice for any manager who is trying to get the best out of a team:

> What is required is that we unite with others, in order that all may complement and aid one another through holding together. But such holding together calls for a central figure around whom other persons may unite. To become a centre of influence holding people together is a grave matter and fraught with great responsibility. It requires greatness of spirit, consistency, and strength. Therefore, let him who wishes to gather others about him ask himself whether he is equal to the undertaking, for anyone attempting the task without a real calling for it only makes confusion worse than if no union at all had taken place.

The *I Ching* is full of similarly interesting observations on the absolute basics of human nature – as long as you don't attempt to use it to superstitiously foretell the future. Understand that the best way to use it is as a way to challenge yourself to ask the right questions and to think seriously about your responses to the advice it gives you, and it can be a worthwhile tool.

THE SPEED READ

I Ching

An ancient Chinese book of divination, which can also be used as a source of advice on moral and proper conduct. From a business point of view, it shouldn't be seen as a way to predict the future, but as a source of reflection on your job, career or business. By being forced to step back and think of the right questions to ask, you may see your choices and conduct in a different light and be forced to confront your inner doubts and fears, while being challenged to find the correct response to those obstacles. Not for the superstitious or the excessively sceptical, but some may find this a useful and interesting tool and a refreshing change from business manuals that claim to know all the answers, because instead it focuses you on your knowledge of your own capabilities and limitations.

The Prince

Niccolò Machiavelli, 1532

The Prince is a classic text on leadership that has passed the test of time, partly because it is a study in pragmatic decision-making. It can be seen as an immoral book, as its core message is that making choices for the sake of morality can be weak and dangerous, but it is probably better to describe it as amoral. Machiavelli certainly has a poor opinion of mankind, describing them as 'fickle, hypocritical and greedy of gain', and this is part of the motivation for his cynical approach.

It was written at a time when Italy consisted of numerous warring city-states, and derives from a genre of books called 'mirrors of princes'. These were mostly fairly stodgy texts written in Latin, purporting to advise princes on the management of their people and territory. Machiavelli, who wanted to see Italy unified as a single country under a strong leader and who dedicated this book to Lorenzo de' Medici, takes a much racier approach, writing in vernacular Italian and scorning the normal tropes of morality and fairness. A typical piece of advice is for the leader to avoid gaining something by force when they could instead gain it by deception. And he suggests that 'it is much safer to be feared than loved because . . . love is preserved by the link of obligation which,

11

owing to the baseness of men, is broken at every opportunity for their advantage; but fear preserves you by a dread of punishment which never fails.'

He also takes a fairly casual approach to promises, observing that, 'The promise given was a necessity of the past: the word broken is a necessity of the present.' Unsurprisingly, much of what Machiavelli wrote has come to be accepted as the basic tenets of politics today, especially the art of deception and false promises. It is common for politicians to promise, 'I will do this in the near future...' only to say, when the time comes, 'I can no longer do this because circumstances have changed...' This kind of placatory but empty promise would be very familiar to Machiavelli.

As a management text, *The Prince* can be compared and contrasted with Sun Tzu's *The Art of War*. Both take an essentially pragmatic approach to leadership but, where Sun Tzu talks often of leaders in a position of relative weakness, Machiavelli's focus is more on the leader who is in a powerful position and his advice is most useful when it comes to maintaining or expanding that power. So it might be seen to be of more use to those in successful, large companies, rather than small companies who need a bit more subtlety and to win affection rather than strike fear into their competitor's hearts.

The book can be roughly divided into three sections. In the first, Machiavelli describes states and leaders in terms of how the power was acquired – whether the leader has inherited their principality or conquered it, how the leader came to power, whether they are occupying a conquered territory or ruling it from fortresses and so on. While this is mostly of interest from a historical point of view, there are some practical lessons here for managers in situations of change – where departments or companies are merged, for instance. Often the employees of a company that has been taken over are fearful of, or hostile to, the new management and this creates very different challenges to the manager with a long-established team.

The second section of the book is largely about being prepared for warfare. As with *The Art of War*, there are lessons here for business people about being prepared at all times for the unforeseen and having a thorough knowledge of the terrain on which they might have to fight (or do business). It is also worth reading Machiavelli's views on mercenaries and considering them with respect to the virtues of a business relying on freelance or permanent staff. Machiavelli has a poor opinion of mercenaries, regarding them as unreliable, and strongly advises the leader to have a standing army which is ready to fight at any time. Obviously, the kind of business you are in dictates the make-up of your personnel, but clearly greater levels of commitment and loyalty are likely to be shown by permanent employees with a stable position.

Machiavelli is not typically bloodthirsty, preferring peaceful solutions to warlike ones, but he does give some fairly ruthless advice on dealing with enemies: 'If an injury has to be done to a man it should be so severe that his vengeance need not be feared.' A line that wouldn't be out of place in *The Godfather*.

The third part of the book contains the most typically 'Machiavellian' pieces of advice, as it focuses more on the personal qualities that a leader should have and, even more crucially, the virtues that he should pretend to have. He gives numerous examples of historical leaders who have attempted to act virtuously and have come a cropper as a result. He writes, 'The way men live is so far removed from the way they ought to live that anyone who abandons what is for what should be pursues his downfall rather than his preservation; for a man who strives after goodness in all his acts is sure to come to ruin, since there are so many men who are not good.' Machiavelli instead promotes self-interest as the route to success.

However, he also stresses the need for a leader to appear to be virtuous to as many people as possible, while bearing in mind that 'a prince who wants to keep his authority must learn how not to be good and use that knowledge, or refrain from using it, as necessity requires'. For Machiavelli, the amoral approach is sometimes the only sensible one and he regards virtue as a cloak that can be used to achieve one's aims and goals.

This can be a fairly depressing approach, especially given how closely many modern corporations appear to follow in his footsteps. But one can read Machiavelli for inspiration without becoming a monster – in many respects his advice is simply about how to make pragmatic decisions and to persuade others to work in your interests. It can also be extremely useful when observing the behaviour of others in the workplace, as it can help you to recognise Machiavellian manoeuvring and defend yourself from the consequences. In this respect, *The Prince* remains a classic, and will do so until all of humanity leads perfectly moral lives and no leader or manager need ever stoop to deception, pretence or dishonesty.

THE SPEED READ

The Prince

'How we live is so different from how we ought to live that he who studies what ought to be done rather than what is done will learn the way to his downfall rather than to his preservation.' The classic sixteenth-century guide to amoral leadership and how to gain, preserve and expand your power, this is unfortunately still a useful read in the modern day because 'the lion cannot protect himself from traps and the fox cannot defend himself from wolves. One must therefore be a fox to recognise traps, and a lion to frighten wolves.'

The Wealth of Nations

Adam Smith, 1776

The science of economics as we know it today has many predecessors, but Adam Smith probably deserves to be credited as its true founder. *The Wealth of Nations* is his masterpiece, in which he introduces the idea of the 'invisible hand' of the free market:

> It is not from the benevolence of the butcher, the brewer, or the baker that we expect our dinner, but from their regard to their own interest . . . He generally, indeed, neither intends to promote the public interest, nor knows how much he is promoting it . . . he intends only his own security; and by directing that industry in such a manner as its produce may be of the greatest value, he intends only his own gain, and he is in this, as in many other cases, led by an invisible hand to promote an end which was no part of his intention.

It's not necessary for a business person to know every detail of economic theory and history, but it would be remiss not to have at least a basic idea of the concept of supply and demand curves, productivity, the division of labour and so forth. And it is with Smith that many of these concepts found their first clear definition.

Of course, as a book from the eighteenth century, it is not always an easy read. Smith has an easy-going writing style and explains most of his points clearly, but there are an awful lot of pages in which he discusses the price of corn in contemporary markets or expounds on the errors of the mercantilists. It's definitely advisable to read this in an abridged version, ideally one with a good introduction and that is well annotated.

His primary focus is the question of what constitutes a nation's wealth – it was widely accepted at the time that this could be measured in precious metals and that it was there-fore in the interests of powerful economies to rig the trading system in their own favour, to boost exports and minimise imports. Smith's insight was that true wealth consisted of the goods and services a nation produced and the capital assets used in that production and that setting trade free of petty constraints would thus increase wealth.

He was also one of the first to clearly make the intellectual case for the division of labour, which would become one of the key features of the factory system through the Industrial Revolution. And by arguing that capital assets were a part of the nation's wealth, he made the case for countries to invest in their own future.

Another theme was that, because market forces operated automatically, driven only by the self-interest of all partici-pants, prices would naturally fall and rise with demand and supply and that governments should restrain from too much regulation and interference in the market. In par-ticular, it should avoid granting monopolies or tax preferences and controls.

He also made the case that the government did need to keep the peace and security, build infrastructure and educate the populace. So while Smith is especially beloved of free-market fundamentalists in the modern world, the economic basics are also in place in his work for those who believe in enlightened regulation and government investment. Smith didn't take the extreme position that a government should be utterly minimal, merely that it should restrict its activities to the right and proper areas and should minimise its interference in the market. And anyone who wants to object to modern capitalism or to dispute the free-market purist ideology should be familiar with Smith, if only to ground their arguments in strong economic foundations.

Since Smith is the founding father of free trade, this is an interesting work to return to in the modern world, when anti-globalisation is on the rise and there is increasing talk of tariffs and protectionism. It is certain he would have been against the latter policies, though he may well also have frowned on the degree to which corporations have been able to capture governments and influence their own regulatory framework (often to the detriment of smaller companies).

You don't need to have read this book to do business in the world today. But the global economy might be very different if it weren't for the ideas expressed in it, and the future shape of the global economy may depend on how we react to the twenty-first-century forms of the very same problems that Smith was commenting on.

The Wealth of Nations

The eighteenth-century classic that laid the foundations of modern economics. Smith outlined the arguments for free trade, the advantages of the division of labour and the need to prevent governments from excessive meddling with the market. This is the book that introduced the idea of the 'invisible hand' of the free market, and should thus be familiar to anyone who wants to understand the political arguments over tariffs, protectionism, corporate power and the future of globalisation.

Extraordinary Popular Delusions and the Madness of Crowds

Charles Mackay, 1841

This is a classic that is worth a few hours of anyone's time. It is a survey of bizarre historical crazes and hysterias, from the South Sea Bubble to witch trials, and from popular belief in haunted houses to the tulip frenzy in Holland, all of which the author recounts with a dry amusement that brings out the weirdness of the human psyche in such situations. It continues to be a fascinating study in human irrationality and market psychology.

There are three reasons why this book is worth reading or rereading from a business point of view. Firstly, it is a valuable guide to the way that hysteria leads to irrational swings in markets and, in particular, to booms, bubbles and crashes. Secondly, it serves as a reminder that even highly intelligent people can get things utterly and disastrously wrong. And thirdly, from a more cynical point of view, knowing how market psychology works, whether in hysterias or fads and fashions, is at the heart of the ability to influence popular opinion and to convey a marketing message effectively.

Taking these in turn, Mackay starts the book with an

examination of financial bubbles, in particular the South Sea Bubble, the Mississippi Scheme and 'tulipomania', in which tulip prices in Holland reached extraordinary levels – to the point where they were, in some cases, worth as much as a decent-sized house or twelve acres of land. (Mackay's account of the latter has since been the subject of some academic criticism that notes he may have exaggerated some of the details – but that doesn't really detract from the humour he extracts from the irrational surge in prices). All of these cases revolve around the buying and selling of assets that experienced an initial surge in prices for perfectly rational reasons, but which then went into a period of hysterical price inflation as greater numbers of participants surged into the market in the belief that prices would continue to rise.

Since the book was written there have been numerous further examples of such irrational bubbles, from Railway Mania of the nineteenth century, through the Wall Street Crash and numerous real-estate bubbles of the twentieth century, to the dot-com crash and, most recently, the global financial crisis of 2008.

The moral of the stories is to be cautious about anything which looks like a safe bet: prices can rise irrationally for a very long time before they crash and it is never easy to distinguish a genuine boom from a bubble, but a knowledge of the many ways in which asset prices have soared and crashed in the past is an essential part of defending oneself against getting sucked into future manias. This applies whether you are investing your money in businesses or making decisions about the future direction of your company. One recent instance is the huge amount of money many major publishing companies lost by piling resources into the production of CD-ROMs just as the internet was about to make them more or less unsaleable. In general, it is all too easy for people to follow the crowd because 'everyone else is doing it' and for greed and fear to provoke irrational business behaviour.

When it comes to the potential for highly intelligent people to make foolish mistakes, there are few better parables than the story of John Law, which is recounted in the first chapter of the book. In the early eighteenth century, Law rose to a prominent position of influence in France, which was suffering from economic problems. A brilliant mathematician, gambler and economist, Law believed he could solve these problems. He was ahead of his time in some respects as he had great faith in paper money (as opposed to gold) and the use of shares and bonds as pseudo-money. Law was given a royal charter which allowed him to establish the Banque Royale, with extraordinary privileges in exchange for the bank taking on the national debt of France. He subsequently helped form the Mississippi Company, which was given a monopoly of trade with the West Indies and North America.

When Law issued 50,000 shares in the company at 500 livres each in 1719, he allowed them to be sold for a downpayment of just 75 livres. (The livre was the precursor of the franc, with a value that had originally been equivalent to a pound of silver). As news of the potential wealth of colonies such as Louisiana was wildly exaggerated, the price of the shares rocketed to twenty times their issue price and a hysteria ensued in which buyers clamoured to get into this amazing market opportunity. Law then proposed to pay off the national debt of 1.5 billion livres through the issue of hundreds of thousands more shares. The price continued to shoot up, and the word 'millionaire' was coined for the first time at the height of the bubble.

Inevitably, the bubble burst in 1720, as food prices rose sharply and doubts gathered about how all this paper money and shares could possibly live up to their extremely high valuation. As people attempted to swap their shares and paper money for gold or coins, the prices of the shares crashed. Riots and bank runs ensued and the bank was forced to stop exchanging the paper money. Law ended his days in exile in Italy: for all his brilliance, he had still made one of economic history's most disastrous mistakes.

(While Law was primarily responsible for the debacle, it is worth noting that some of his ideas would eventually become part of mainstream economics and, indeed, contemporary central banking practice: he might even be called the father of quantitative easing. Whether that should tell us that being right at the wrong time is as bad as being plain wrong, or should give us grave concerns about the future of the global economy, is a moot point.)

The final message one can take from Mackay's book is the most cynical one. Given that humans can behave in deeply irrational ways and are subject to fads and fashions, one of the challenges facing a business is how to take advantage of that irrationality (and how to avoid having it undermine your business model). It is not much use manufacturing a wonderful product if you are unable to persuade people of its virtues: marketing and an understanding of market psychology are one of the most basic attributes a business person requires.

In this respect the book is prescient – in later chapters Mackay discusses such things as the strange variation of fashions in men's beards (and how this related to current events), the veneration of famous criminals and the way that big cities can experience a sudden rise and fall in certain catchphrases or songs. These days we might talk about 'the tipping point' (see p. 138), memes going viral, the peculiar fashion crazes of hipsters and others, and the ways in which 'fake news' is circulated in a 'post-truth' world, but we would essentially be talking about the same subjects covered in this book. We would all like to have a business which relies only on rational purchase decisions, but it is never a bad idea to also understand how irrational consumers and opinions can be and to take that into account in our business and marketing plans. Nor is it a bad idea to be reminded of how quickly trends can change and that we might need to adapt or risk failing in the future.

THE SPEED READ

Extraordinary Popular Delusions and the Madness of Crowds

People are strange. Sometimes they behave completely irrationally, especially when they are driven by greed and fear. This book gathers from previous centuries some bizarre, hilarious and salutary examples of irrational behaviour by mobs, crowds and populations, in particular, economic bubbles and manias. A brilliant, frequently hilarious reminder of human frailty and how quickly things can change.

The Principles of
Scientific Management

Frederick Winslow Taylor, 1911

This book is often mentioned on business courses as a historic example of the Efficiency Movement and the transformation of industrial methods in the early twentieth century, but is not so often actually read. It has become something of a period piece, because so much of the language and ideas are quaint, peculiar or dated. However, it is a fascinating read and one that throws light on the way that things have changed in the century since it was written.

Frederick Winslow Taylor was a mechanical engineer who was obsessed with the concept of efficiency. Early in the book he points out that there was a lot of attention being paid to the waste of natural resources, but less being paid to the waste of human resources that was the result of inefficient industrial methods. He disparages the idea that these can be achieved by looking for 'the right man for the job', arguing that

> What we are all looking for, however, is the ready-made, competent man; the man whom someone else has trained. It is only when we fully realise that our duty, as well as our

25

opportunity, lies in systematically cooperating to train and to make this competent man, instead of in hunting for a man whom some one else has trained, that we shall be on the road to national efficiency.

It's notable that Taylor was not only an early advocate of the idea that national productivity was important, but also that he had such a strong focus on training (something that is often sadly lacking in today's world of outsourcing and globalisation). But he didn't just think that workers needed to be trained efficiently – he also believed that it was necessary to teach managers how to manage, and as such he can be seen as one of the earliest management consultants. He continues:

In the past the prevailing idea has been well expressed in the saying that 'Captains of industry are born, not made'; and the theory has been that if one could get the right man, methods could be safely left to him.

Instead Taylor's aim was to set out a systematic, scientific approach to management which would do away with the idea of the 'great man' of industry and instead lead to the best possible organisation of any group of managers and workers (while arguing that such a system would also encourage the best potential managers to rise to the surface).

His methods for achieving this were largely based on his observations of the steel industry and his rather condescendingly expressed view that most workers spent their time 'soldiering' (slacking deliberately so as not to get the work done too quickly.) He felt that workers soldiered because they felt a social pressure not to do other men out of work.

Taylor had a range of remedies for this. Firstly, he was a big fan of the time-and-motion approach to industrial practices and felt that, for instance, one could identify the exact right kind of shovel, shovel-load of coal and number of rest periods a day that would achieve maximum efficiency.

Secondly, he felt that workers needed to be persuaded out of their reluctance by having it explained to them that increased productivity would actually mean lower prices, higher demand, and thus more work all round. (Which, up to a point, is true although it ignores displaced effects on other parts of the industry.) And he also advocated making sure that workers received part of the fruit of increased efficiency in the form of higher wages – in that respect Taylor actually comes across as more enlightened than many modern corporations, given that we have seen wages stagnate through decades of productivity growth. This is in spite of the fact that Taylor is remembered for treating workers harshly, as mere commodities that should be exploited as efficiently as possible.

It is fascinating to read how often Taylor emphasises the need for workers and management to co-operate and to share the load. However, this is undermined by passages in which he makes fun of individual workers as being clumsy or stupid (even mocking the accent of an immigrant worker at one point) and makes statements such as, 'This work is so crude and elementary in its nature that the writer firmly believes that it would be possible to train an intelligent gorilla so as to become a more efficient pig-iron handler than any man can be.'

So this isn't a book that should be read for pertinent, modern advice, but as a fascinating window into a time by which modern industrial practices had not fully evolved, workers were still using oddly assorted shovels that they brought to the factory themselves, and constant surveillance of employees to ensure they met their daily targets was still a weird dystopian future vision. Albeit this vision was one that Taylor helped to bring a few steps closer through his noble commitment to the cause of efficiency.

┌─ **THE SPEED READ** ─────────────────────────────────┐

The Principles of Scientific Management

In the brave new world of the early twentieth century, we need to develop new industrial practices which place efficiency at the heart of the business. We need to train managers to apply scientific principles, such as studying the most efficient way each worker can move a pile of pig-iron, and we need to convince those silly workers that their best interests are not served by deliberately working slowly, as they so often do in our factories. In the future, increased efficiency will be good for everyone, workers and managers alike, as they share together in permanent prosperity for all.

└──┘

How to Win Friends and Influence People

Dale Carnegie, 1936

If you ever get the question 'What do Warren Buffett and Charles Manson have in common?' in a quiz, the answer may be that the billionaire investor and murderous gang-leader are allegedly both fans of *How to Win Friends and Influence People* by Dale Carnegie. It's a strange pairing, but it indicates a dichotomy that lies at the heart of this classic self-help book, as we shall see.

The way in which the first publication of the book in 1936 came about is itself a parable of good business sense. The self-help genre barely existed at the time. Carnegie was giving extremely popular classes on public speaking in New York when Leon Shimkin of the publishing house Simon & Schuster approached him and asked if he would consider turning his lessons into a book – Shimkin thought that he had spotted a gap in the market and he wasn't wrong. The book was hugely successful from the start and has gone on to sell well over thirty million copies around the world. (Publishers generally need a few of these kinds of successes now and then to underwrite the many less successful books they will publish in between.)

The book presents itself as a guide to everyday action. Carnegie uses a lot of homespun wisdom, quotes from Ralph Waldo Emerson, the American writer and philospher, and parables of ordinary folk who changed the way they dealt with people and went on to great success. His main focus is on positive thinking and how to get on with people and change their behaviour in the process.

He advises the reader to show genuine interest in other people, and to try to empathise with their point of view and also to smile and to remember to use their names: he describes a person's name as the sweetest and most important sound they can hear. He also stresses the advantages of being a good listener, of framing any problem in terms of the other person's interests and making them feel important.

There are two criticisms that are often levelled at the book: firstly that it is trite, and secondly that it is a manual on manipulation rather than genuinely acquiring friends. Carnegie had been a modestly successful salesman (who changed his name from Carnagey to the more opulent-sounding Carnegie) and an unsuccessful actor before he started giving the lectures and it is easy to see how this history influenced his advice – it is questionable whether you would really acquire friends by doing everything he says, as friends are those with whom one has a more sincere and deep relationship. His advice is more obviously aimed at someone in a business environment dealing with customers, clients or suppliers.

On this level, there is a danger of sounding like a cheesy used-car salesman if you slavishly put his principles into practice. Constant smiling, gratuitous use of the other person's name and clumsy wielding of anecdotes could easily come across as smarmy and duplicitous. But many readers have instead applied the basic principles of empathy, interest, avoiding excessive criticism and being willing to criticise oneself and have done this in ways that work within their own culture and time. For instance, Warren Buffett's appreciation of the book is rooted in his ability to listen to Carnegie's underlying message and adapt it to his own way of doing business.

When it comes to the second criticism, that the book teaches you how to manipulate people rather than befriend them, it should be acknowledged that, according to a recent biography, Charles Manson valued the book for the ability it gave him to persuade people to do things they didn't want to – even to get someone to kill another for him.

On a less murderous level, President Bill Clinton was renowned for remembering people's names and stories when he had met them only briefly years before and it can seem like a mere trick when you discover that this was because he kept meticulous box files in which he noted down such information. On the other hand, those people for whom he always had a friendly word still found themselves impressed by what came across as a genuine interest; they were flattered by the attention and recognition from this powerful man, regardless of the means by which he achieved this feat.[1]

It is worth quoting Carnegie here: he sometimes expresses quite a poor opinion of human nature, writing, for instance, that 'people are not interested in you. They are not interested in me. They are interested in themselves – morning, noon and after dinner.' This is the fundamental reason he advises the reader to show interest in others, because that is what will be most persuasive. And while warning the reader against succumbing to flattery themselves, much of

---

[1] David Maraniss, *First in His Class: A Biography of Bill Clinton*, Pocket Books, New York, 1996, p. 260

his advice appears to encourage them to flatter others for their own gains.

Carnegie does address this issue – he makes the distinction that flattery is insincere whereas genuine appreciation is sincere. And he tells the reader that the principles in the book will only work for them if they follow them 'from the heart'. But there is a tension here between Carnegie's unsympathetic description of people as essentially self-absorbed and the goal of genuinely appreciating them. Readers who respond most strongly to the negative description of humanity, as Charles Manson apparently did, can find the book works as a guide to insincere manipulation. Whereas those who accept Carnegie was sincere in his direction to show genuine appreciation in others and to do so from the heart will find the book a more positive and uplifting read.

Some of the value of the book lies in relatively small details. For managers, the section on how to persuade other people to change their actions and opinions contains some gems. For instance, Carnegie advises the reader to always ask questions rather than give orders, so that the listener can come to the desired conclusion on their own rather than feeling coerced. And his advice to influence others by giving them a good example to live up to is as important today as it was eighty years ago.

One other warning: while it was updated in later editions, in places the material is seriously dated, especially the homilies about individuals who improved their own lives, which can be squirmingly embarrassing to a modern reader. However, if you approach this book with a positive attitude and an open heart, it may still provide a useful mirror through which to evaluate your own relationships with others, especially in the workplace, and to improve your powers of persuasion and empathy.

How to Win Friends and Influence People

People are most interested in themselves, so if you want them to like you, or want to sell them ideas or products, you need to show genuine interest in them and to see things from their point of view. Smile, use their name, listen to them, explain problems in terms that will make sense from their perspective, be a good listener. Don't criticise or condemn and readily admit to your own mistakes. Start out by asking questions to which they can easily answer 'Yes' and encourage them to talk themselves round to your point of view. And soon they will be happy and falling over themselves to buy whatever it is you have to sell to them. They might even kill someone for you.

Think and Grow Rich

Napoleon Hill, 1937

If you want an example of everything that can be wrong with a business title, look no further than Napoleon Hill's *Think and Grow Rich,* a book that embodies the most infuriating and dishonest characteristics of the genre and which prefigures many of the worst books to be found later in this collection.

As his starting point, Hill described a meeting that he had with the rich US industrialist Andrew Carnegie in 1908, after which he apparently spent many years meeting with the nation's most successful men, including US presidents Franklin Delano Roosevelt and Woodrow Wilson (to whom he claimed to have been an adviser) and Henry Ford. He had boiled down the wisdom he had gained from these men into a series of booklets known as *The Law of Success* in the 1920s, but in *Think and Grow Rich,* published in the dark days of the Great Depression, he condensed this material down into his Philosophy of Achievement. This consisted of thirteen principles, which included obvious virtues such as Desire, Faith and Persistence alongside some nuttier ideas such as Autosuggestion, the Power of the Mastermind and even the Mystery of Sex Transmutation. The meaning of the last point is a bit unclear, since it can be taken either to mean you should transform your sexual energy and channel it elsewhere or that the rich males Hill had met had a tendency to be a bit oversexed and frisky. It's probably not worth pausing too long to worry about which is the correct interpretation.

Hill's basic message is that you can become rich if you want it really, really badly. You need to focus completely on the method you have chosen to achieve this, which you should write down and reread morning, noon and night. This will then transmute itself via your subconscious mind, which vibrates with something called the Infinite Intelligence and affects the material world. Lots of people had peculiar ideas in his period, of course, and there are some practical suggestions as well, although mostly focused on determination and impressing other people. Finally, he speaks of a great secret, which he had previously identified as the Golden Rule, but which here seems to refer to your ability to shape the universe to your desires through sheer force of willpower. (This has led some people to see this as the forerunner of the 2006 best-selling film and book *The Secret* by Rhonda Byrne, which made similarly woolly, mystical claims about the path to success.)

It has to be accepted that this book was hugely successful and has many fans who still swear by its virtues. At heart its message is simply that you can succeed if you want something, believe in your ability to achieve it, do something about it and keep persisting. You might hear similar opinions from the mouth of Donald Trump (who has spoken warmly of his childhood pastor, Norman Vincent Peale, author of the 1952 book *The Power of Positive Thinking* and apparently a disciple of Hill himself). And for some people such words can be a genuine inspiration to success.

Let's ignore Hill's appeal to mystical nonsense, like the concept that riches always begin in ideas which are a product of thought vibrations in the ether. There are so many better reasons to dislike this book – its contradictions, its trite lists and checkpoints, its claims of validation via earlier success stories, its simplistic approach to the concept of 'achievement' and its appeal to naked greed in its readers, along with the idea that this greed will lead to its own satisfaction. (A typical Hill quote: 'The starting point of all achievements is desire. Keep this constantly in mind. Weak desire brings weak results, just as a small fire makes a small amount of heat.')

In addition, there is not much evidence that Hill's claims about the birth of the book are true in the first place (some have suggested that he was a bit of a huckster and a charlatan). He may never have met Andrew Carnegie (none of his writings made this claim until after Carnegie's death), probably wasn't ever a presidential adviser and quite possibly didn't meet all those rich famous guys at all.

If he was making it up, maybe we should see him as an amusing conman and forgive him for his chutzpah. Either way, the truly pernicious thing about this book is the influence it has had on decades of self-help and business books that followed, the worst of which take a single dubious idea and overinflate it while adding lists of spurious 'principles' or 'laws' and sure-fire ways to success. The best of the books in this collection (such as *The Efficient Executive* or *Getting to Yes*) are those that take a more complex approach, rooted in genuine experience or research. In the end, those are the books that deserve to be called business classics, not exploitative moonshine like *Think and Grow Rich*.

Think and Grow Rich

Do you want to be rich? Do you really, really want to be rich? DO YOU REALLY??? Then listen up – I've almost definitely, certainly toured the nation over many years speaking to rich and famous men and have distilled their wisdom into thirteen principles that add up to what I like to call my Philosophy of Achievement. If you want that big car, that beautiful spouse, that huge mansion, you need to think, think, think about it, then through mystical vibrations in the air you will come into contact with the Infinite Intelligence and magically an idea or hunch will come to you. And ALL RICHES START FROM IDEAS. Then you need to keep wanting it, keep working, keep persisting. You need to transmute that sexual energy, unleash the power of the Mastermind, and you need to USE CAPITALS WHEN YOU ARE EMPHASISING YOUR MOST FATUOUS POINTS. And never forget this, there really is a secret to getting rich and if you just give me all your money I promise I will tell you all about it.

The Intelligent Investor

Benjamin Graham, 1949

Benjamin Graham is a legend in the world of professional investment, revered by Warren Buffett and Irving Kahn, among many other successful investors. His two best-known books are *Security Analysis* and *The Intelligent Investor* and, while the former has much to recommend it in terms of detailed advice on how to analyse companies, the latter has probably been the most influential.

Graham is credited with inventing the concept of value investing, a subject he taught about at Columbia Business School from the late 1920s onwards. He was an advocate of using objective measures of the value of a company's shares, and removing emotion or subjective judgements from the picture. To this end he developed a range of rules and measures which the investor could use to find value investments. His books give detailed breakdowns of ways in which the investor could analyse a company's performance, but the most basic rule was to look for companies where the stock price gives you a margin of safety. By this he meant that there was a significant difference between the stock's current value and its intrinsic value. If a stock had a good margin of safety, with a higher intrinsic value than the current value, he regarded it as more likely to withstand downturns in the market and, more importantly for him, was more likely to provide a good income.

He was an advocate of genuine investment rather than speculation and saw stockholders as sharing in the owner-ship of a company – he disapproved of the growing tendency for shares to be treated as casino chips and for their owners to take no interest in how the company was being run. His approach to investment relied more on holding stocks for the long term and spreading investment across a range of companies that fit his criteria, arguing that 'the real money in investment will have to be made – as most of it has been in the past – not out of buying and selling but of owning and holding securities, receiving interest and dividends and increases in value'.

It has to be remembered that the index fund didn't exist when Graham was writing (see *Common Sense on Mutual Funds* p.118), but much of his advice has come to fruition in the use of such funds. He argued that matching the perfor-mance of the overall market should be regarded as a reasonable expectation and pointed out the absurdity of a market full of fund managers who all claim to be able to beat the average. For this reason he argued that investors should always hold a diversified range of stocks and view the long-term perfor-mance as being the best measure of intelligent investing.

One parable he used in his lectures concerned a person called Mr Market, who knocked on your door every day offering to sell you shares at random prices. Sometimes the price would seem right, sometimes it would seem too high or too low. His point was not to get too caught up in the swings and roundabouts of market sentiment but to patiently compare the price of Mr Market to intrinsic value.

Warren Buffett, who describes his approach to investing as being 85 per cent derived from Graham, continues to advocate some of the analysis tools set out in Graham's books. For instance, one way to judge a company is to look at how sensibly it is investing in its own future. If the retained earnings over a five-year period are lower than the increase in share value (assuming the five-year period doesn't start or end in a particular boom or bust) then you can judge that the company is investing its cash wisely and, since the cash could otherwise be returned to stockholders, you can judge that they are looking after your money well. This is the kind of simple but profound advice that marks Graham's approach out – it seems pretty obvious to say that you should only trust a company with your money if they are going to look after it better than you could, but it can take years of investing and market-watching to boil your approach down to such simple but valuable rules.

Graham's approach to risk focused on the distinction between passive and active investors. For passive investors who didn't want to devote too much time to analysis, he recommended a more cautious approach, arguing that the apparently riskier investments only made sense for those investors who had done their homework very carefully. He often castigated companies for issuing opaque and confusing financial results, a problem that has only got worse since his day.

In some other respects his advice can seem somewhat dated, if only because so much investing is now instant and carried out online. There is also a debate to be had about whether there is really such a thing as intrinsic value – common sense suggests that share prices are sometimes too high or too low, but the efficient markets hypothesis (for those who believe in it) suggests otherwise.

However, the fundamentals of investment never really change and Benjamin Graham is one of the wisest teachers you could look to if you want to find objective, intelligent ways to invest your money. His approach may be boringly conservative, but it has worked for many investors over the years and will continue to do so in future.

THE SPEED READ

The Intelligent Investor

If you want to invest your money intelligently, do not pay too much attention to the vagaries of Mr Market. Instead, focus on investment rather than speculation, analyse company financials carefully and aim to at least match market performance by investing in a diverse range of companies, selected using a simple range of tools and measures. If you want to devote more time to understanding the companies you invest in, you may be able to profit from taking larger risks, otherwise remain cautious in your approach. Bear in mind that as a shareholder you own part of the company and should expect clear financial results, sensible management and a good approach to investing in the company's future. Invest for the long term and aim to make money from the interest and dividends, not just from increases in share value. Always focus on buying stocks with a margin of safety, where the share price is lower than the intrinsic value, and you will put yourself in a good position to profit in the medium to long term.

Parkinson's Law or
The Pursuit of Progress

C. Northcote Parkinson, 1958

Parkinson's Law is the satirical scientific rule that 'work expands so as to fill the time available for its completion'. It was formulated by C. Northcote Parkinson, a British naval historian, in an essay he wrote for the *Economist* magazine in 1955 that was subsequently reissued as the main essay in a book of the same name in 1958.

The book is short and tongue-in-cheek, and focuses on parochial British subject matter such as the best time to arrive at a cocktail party and the inner workings of the civil service (although it was also popular in the communist bloc, where they had their own painful experiences of malign bureaucracy). However, this doesn't detract from its powerful satire of how organisations work, much of which will be easily recognised by anyone who has ever sat in too many weekly meetings or wondered why staffing levels in their organisation keep growing regardless of performance.

The basic law is based on observations of how officials or managers tend to behave, in particular if they feel that they are overworked. Parkinson notes that very few managers will either resign (in acknowledgment that they aren't up to the job any more) or share their work with someone of equal status (who they will see as a competitor). Instead they will prefer to delegate the work to subordinates and, rather than hiring one junior staff member, they will be inclined to hire two, each of whom has a separate area of responsibility (meaning that neither of them are a suitable challenger for his own role).

Subsequently each of those juniors may in turn feel over-worked and will choose the same method of dealing with it – when each of them has two juniors, the original role that was filled by one person has expanded so that seven people are now working on it.

At this stage a second problem kicks in – people in companies tend to make work for each other. In the original essay Parkinson gives an example of a letter that needs to be written. Rather than draft it himself, the first official will delegate it to official B, who will ask one of his juniors to prepare a draft. The draft will be circulated with various members of the group spending time rereading, checking and proposing more or less suitable amendments. In the end the letter will be passed to the first official, who will spend as much time revising it as he would have spent writing the damn thing in the first place. It has taken seven people to achieve the same output as one person might.

(It's worth noting also that this kind of process is also a way for each employee to deflect part of the responsibility for the task and thus reduce their own stress levels – which may make their lives easier, but is problematic from the company's point of view as it makes it less likely for any individual to truly take responsibility.)

Of course, in these days of ruthless streamlining and down-sizing, this portrait of how companies work may look like a relic from the past. However, Parkinson's ire was largely directed at bureaucracies and even today civil services the world over continue to employ thousands of workers and expand way beyond any necessity. And there have been numerous updates to Parkinson's Law that will ring true for anyone engaged in business today. For instance, the Stock-Sanford corollary to Parkinson's Law dictates that if you leave something to the last minute, it will only take a minute to do it. And in computer science, it has been observed that data tends to expand to fill the space available for storage.

In elaborating on the law, Parkinson gave examples from the UK civil service in which the bureaucracy tended to grow at a regular rate of about 5–6 per cent a year regardless. For instance, from 1914 to 1928 the Admiralty, the administrative branch responsible for the Navy, grew from 2,000 to about 3,500 officials, in spite of the actual Navy shrinking by over a half in the same period. And while Parkinson notes the possibility that technical change had made this necessary, he notes that administrators increased by significantly more than technicians in this period. Similarly, the Colonial Office grew by about four times between 1935 and 1954 in spite of the number of British colonies they had to deal with shrinking hugely in the same period.

As well as his law, Parkinson made numerous other astute observations of how organisations can go wrong. He noted that just as companies tend to expand in size, so do individual committees or meeting groups. And using examples from British history, he demonstrates how the maximal size for a meeting or committee is about three to ten people – any growth beyond that point will lead to discussion being disrupted, confused and indecisive as too many people have the opportunity to poke their oar in or start separate private conversations within the meeting. This is a problem which afflicts any growing company as decision-making units tend also to expand. More senior staff feel the need to be in on all discussions.

He also outlines another useful rule, Parkinson's Law of Triviality, by describing a committee that has to make two decisions about construction projects, one for an atomic reactor and the other for a bike shed. He points out that it will tend to be the trivial item on the agenda that eats up the most time because 'a reactor is so vastly expensive and complicated that an average person cannot understand it, so one assumes that those who work on it understand it. On the other hand, everyone can visualise a cheap, simple bicycle shed, so planning one can result in endless discussions because everyone involved wants to add a touch and show personal contribution.'

If you can get past the fact that the book is rooted in very local examples from the 1950s, this is still a terrific satire of how companies malfunction, and it is painfully accurate when it comes to the ways in which meetings and committees can tie themselves in knots and expend huge amounts of energy on making the wrong decision, in the wrong way and at the wrong time.

THE SPEED READ

Parkinson's Law or The Pursuit of Progress

Bureaucracies (and companies) tend to expand at a fairly constant rate, regardless of whether this is necessary. This is for two main reasons: firstly, officials and managers prefer hiring subordinates to rivals and prefer to divide their delegated work between more than one junior in order to avoid either of them building up a base from which to challenge their position. Secondly, officials and employees make work for each other, the same documents will pass through more hands, there is more creation of spurious work such as progress meetings, budget target documents and assessments. So the work will expand to take up the employee hours available for its completion. Committees and steering groups will similarly expand to unwieldy proportions until they become ineffectual and all committees will tend to focus on trivial problems rather than major ones. And for all these reasons companies and bureaucracies have a natural tendency to become less efficient over time, not more.

The Effective Executive

Peter Drucker, 1967

Peter Drucker is one of the most interesting twentieth-century thinkers on the subject of management. The author of many books on business, from his first in 1939 through to a posthumous title published in 2008, he examined how people work with businesses from many different angles. Following his work with General Motors in the 1940s, he advised businesses on their management practices. He was the first to coin the term 'knowledge worker' as early as 1959 and was prescient in seeing how important such work would become. He was also among the first to predict the decline of blue-collar work in first-world economies such as the USA.

In his later years, he was an evangelist for outsourcing – he wrote a 1989 *Wall Street Journal* article called 'Sell the Mailroom' and advised businesses to 'do what you do best and outsource the rest'.[1] In the current climate in which there has been a backlash against outsourcing and other effects of globalisation, this may not seem like his most appealing feature.

---

[1] Peter Drucker, 'Sell the Mailroom', *Wall Street Journal*, 25 July 1989

However, he should be remembered more warmly for his earlier work in which he focused strongly on the human side of business and tried to understand how differing personalities could be harnessed together to work for the common good through business. He always looked for the best in people and believed that companies could be noble enterprises that made the world a better place. He also rejected the idea that a company's primary purpose was to make profit, preferring to argue that its main task was to serve its customers.

The Effective Executive, a book which Amazon founder Jeff Bezos apparently asks his senior management team to read, is one of the best examples of his writing. It was first published in 1967 but is full of advice and observations that are as relevant today as they were then. The core of Drucker's argument is that the most important thing for managers to learn is the habit of effective behaviour and that this is a habit that can be acquired through practice. The subtitle of the book – 'the definitive guide to getting the right things done' – is crucial in this respect; Drucker isn't just telling managers how to get things done (or even, as many managers seem to want, to *appear* to be getting things done), but to get the *right* things done.

He breaks this down into five segments. The first is to know how you are spending your time – time-management being a practice that is best learned through personal application. By knowing how your time is spent you will be better placed to consider how each different activity you engage in is affecting the business and how effective you are actually being. A manager can be in many meetings a day and spend a lot of time writing reports without actually achieving anything. Drucker wisely says, 'There is nothing so useless as doing efficiently that which should not be done at all,' and suggests that you evaluate activities and aim to eliminate any that 'need not be done', 'could be done by others', or are simply 'wasting other people's time'. (The last of those in particular will be music to the ears of anyone who has suffered from an overzealous but incompetent manager – which probably includes most people reading this book.)

Drucker is particularly harsh on the problems of useless information and the way it can proliferate in a company. In modern terms, if too much of your time is being spent reading emails copied to you, you will know you have a problem of information overload. And the same can be said of other pieces of 'organisation' that have been created for no obvious purpose, including unnecessary paperwork or forms to be completed, and pointless interim 'feedback meetings'.

The second step is to focus on what contribution you are actually making. To measure this you need to focus on the external effects of your activities and to aim high to bring out the best in yourself.

Thirdly, you need to focus on your strengths. One of Drucker's endearing qualities is that he recognises that everyone has different skills and abilities. Rather than forcing square pegs into round holes, he suggests that companies look for ways to fit everyone's special abilities into a greater whole. And if you are to achieve this as a manager, the first place to start is by recognising your personal strengths and weaknesses, since it is more effective to work to your strengths than to try to improve on weaknesses. And when evaluating the qualities of employees and colleagues, it is important to remember that they are not always as obvious as it may seem. 'The most important thing in communication is to hear what isn't being said.'

The fourth aim is to focus on a small number of areas in the company where an improved performance will make the most significant difference. To take a petty example: if you spend two weeks of your year focusing on cutting down on waste in the mailroom and that time could have been spent expanding your export business by 10 per cent, you were probably using your time on the wrong thing.

Finally, Drucker focuses on effective decision-making. He suggests that decisions tend not to be effective if they can't be challenged by others or debated in an effective way (although this also shouldn't mean that decisions get bogged down in too many layers of authorisation and discussion). He suggests setting out the terms of how to judge the effectiveness of a decision in advance and going back after the event to assess how effective your decisions have actually been. From this you can learn from both your good and bad ideas.

Drucker also points out something that is too often forgotten by managers around the world. When you are making a decision, you should not assume that the outcome has to be action. Sometimes doing nothing really is the best option.

THE SPEED READ

The Effective Executive

Effective management is a habit that can be learned. Managers of modern businesses and institutions are largely responsible for the common good so their performance is hugely important: 'Management is doing things right; leadership is doing the right things.'

To be effective, first analyse how you spend your time at work and seek to eliminate the pointless uses of your time. Measure your external contribution to the company and aim high. Build on your strengths (and those of others) as this will achieve more than focusing on your weaknesses. Focus on the areas of your business where a better performance will make the biggest difference. And above all, aim to make effective decisions and to be honest with yourself about how effective your past decisions have been

The Peter Principle

Why Things Always Go Wrong

Laurence J. Peter, 1969

The Peter Principle is a management theory explained in the drily humorous book of the same name by Laurence J. Peter, a Canadian educator. At its simplest, the principle states that an employee or manager will be promoted to the level of their incompetence. The reasoning behind it is that people tend to be promoted when they make a success of the job they are doing and thus will continue to be promoted until they reach a level at which they are a failure. They will then duly become stuck at that level since they will no longer merit promotion.

A corollary to this is that most of the useful work that gets done in a company is achieved by people who have not yet reached the level of their incompetence. Peter also allows for the possibility that some people at the other end of the bell curve of competence, those who are super-competent, will fail to be promoted at all, since those in superior positions will see them as a threat.

As an analysis of what goes wrong in companies, most people will acknowledge that there is some truth in all of this. Indeed, the principle has been expanded in various ways by other writers since the original book. The generalised principle extends the idea to wider contexts, arguing that anything can be subject to the Peter Principle because a tool, system or method that has proved useful in the past will be employed until it lets the user down. Meanwhile, in IT circles the Peter Principle is used to describe a project that has become so overcomplicated that it is no longer even understood by the people who are working on it.

Peter had a wider interest in 'hierarchiology', a phrase he coined to describe the sociological study of human organisations with a hierarchical structure. Part of his theory focuses on the ways that people acquire specific skills that come naturally to them. For instance, someone might be a brilliant engineer. But when that same person is asked to move up to managing an engineering department, they might prove to have poor interpersonal and managerial skills (and will thus have reached their 'level of incompetence').

The book itself is quite short and genuinely funny. However, it does also prefigure many later business books of more serious intent, in that it stretches out one fairly slender idea over too many pages and thus falls victim to a bit of repetition and padding. And from a more serious point of view, one can argue with a model that states that employees are generally promoted for being competent or successful or that incompetent workers are never promoted.

For an alternative humorous take on the problem, it's worth comparing the Peter Principle with the Dilbert Principle (see p. 99), which takes a different angle on the same problem. But most people will recognise that the Peter Principle does describe some real-world situations pretty accurately, and it's an entertaining read either way.

THE SPEED READ

The Peter Principle

Since people tend to be promoted within organisations when they prove to be competent or successful, they will usually keep getting promoted until they reach a level at which they are unable to be either competent or successful. At this point we can say that they have reached the level of their incompetence, which is where most people will end up in their careers. The only reason companies get any real work done is because of the workers or managers who have not yet been promoted to the level where they are of no use to anyone. As a result, not much will ever go right and plenty of things will go wrong, whether it be in business, in life or in the world in general.

Small is Beautiful

A Study of Economics as if People Mattered

E. F. Schumacher, 1973

A collection of essays by E. F. Schumacher originally published at the height of the oil crisis, in the early days of globalisation, it called for a completely different approach to the problems of economics. This would be one in which sustainability was more important than economic growth and we measured happiness as well as profit.

It is an interesting read which has been hugely influential on environmentalism and alternative economics in the intervening years. But it is also worth a mention because it can also be seen as an influence on the kinds of smaller, sustainable start-ups that are increasingly common in the twenty-first century.

We are accustomed to the idea that efficiency requires economies of scale and that it is logical for all business to grow ever larger through growth, mergers or acquisitions. (And arguably we have become used to the idea that this means an ever richer, global super-elite). However, this isn't always the healthiest approach.

In the early twentieth century, those opposed to capitalism fell into numerous factions, including the Marxists who were believers in large-scale statism. But there were also thinkers like the distributists who had a strong belief that businesses and government should always work at the smaller scale. Schumacher echoed such thinking, advocating 'lots and lots of small autonomous units' as the way forward for the economy. He added a strong environmental note, expressing concern that the world would be unable to rely on continually diminishing reserves of non-renewables.

It's worth noting that Schumacher wasn't entirely focused on 'smallness' as the sole measure of business, as he acknowledged that larger organisations could become more 'human' by operating with smaller units within the whole. For instance, he wrote, 'Organisations should imitate nature, which doesn't allow a single cell to become too large ... The great achievement of [CEO] Mr Sloan of General Motors was to structure this gigantic firm in such a manner that it became in fact a federation of fairly reasonably sized firms.'

Of course, some of Schumacher's concerns have found their way into mainstream thinking – for instance, the widespread use of recycling and increasing concern about disposable packaging in the world today. And the idea of small-scale lending into microbusinesses has played a significant role in the rejuvenation of economies such as that of India. But in other respects the crises of the early twenty-first century mirror those of the 1970s – diminishing stocks of fossil fuels, environmental catastrophes, unstable currencies and global conditions. And the solutions offered by many governments, corporations and multinational organisations still seem to be bereft of imagination and foresight.

He may not appeal to everyone, but for those interested in how to apply business principles on a smaller scale, or who believe that the primary purpose of a business shouldn't necessarily be profit (nor the primary aim of a government 'economic growth'), Schumacher can still be an inspiring read.

THE SPEED READ

Small is Beautiful

Modern Western economies, with their reliance on disposables, fossil fuels and economies of scale, are not sustainable – and teaching developing economies to mimic them will not solve this problem. Rather than striving for constant growth we should be happy with 'enough' and look for small-scale solutions – the economy of the village or local community rather than large-scale industrial processes. In the future, such small-scale economic activity will become more crucial and we should be building those business models now. We should also measure the success of our economy by the health, happiness and well-being of the population, not just the growth in macroeconomic measures.

Getting to Yes

Negotiating Agreement Without Giving In

Roger Fisher and William Ury, 1981

M any people end up in a career without having studied the basic nuts and bolts of business practice. And even among those with business qualifications it is surprising how few have specifically studied the art of negotiation. As a result they learn their negotiation methods through trial and error and rarely manage to take a step back to explore how they can improve on them.

Getting to Yes is the ideal title for anyone who engages in any kind of negotiation at work. Which is basically everyone who has a job of any sort, since negotiation starts at the interview for a job or the pitch for a piece of work and continues through the process of agreeing a fee, salary or working conditions and so on. (And even people without a job negotiate on a regular basis, whether they are persuading a child to tidy their room, taking a faulty product back to the shop or debating rules for a shared house.)

More specifically, it is an excellent resource for anyone who regularly deals with any kind of contract, licence, customer, supplier or subcontractor. The authors were both founding members of the Harvard Negotiation Project.

They have a strong focus on 'principled negotiation' or 'non-adversarial bargaining'. In pursuit of this aim, they start by inviting the negotiator to evaluate which of the aims of the parties involved are fixed and which are flexible. This single piece of advice is a valuable one as we too often overlook areas where the party we are negotiating with may be willing to compromise while fixating on areas where there is simply no progress that can be made. Working out what each party really truly won't budge on and what they may be willing to bargain away should be the starting point for any negotiation.

Fisher and Ury break the general process of principled negotiation into five stages. First, they advise the reader to 'separate the person from the problem' – to refuse to allow negotiations to become personalised and instead to focus on the problem that we are trying to solve. The aim is to avoid feeling that a negotiation is something that you will either win or lose and instead to look at it as a mutual problem that you need to solve together. In particular, it is useful for the negotiator to think about the position of the other party and to think about the problem from their point of view, in order to have a more empathetic understanding of how a solution may be found.

To this end, they then instruct us to 'focus on interests, not positions'. One of the book's few weaknesses is that it doesn't define these terms as rigorously as it might, but the general idea is that a position is an explicit, concrete decision, whereas an interest is the cause or motivation of a position. For instance, it's one thing to know that 'Eve wants a cake' but we have a better understanding of her position if we know whether she is hungry, looking for a present for a friend or in need of cake for her work colleagues.

The next step is to 'invent options for mutual gain'. In other words, rather than focusing narrowly on the immediate problem, it can be immensely useful to think of other possible ways that the interests of each party can be served. As part of this, it is important to look for items that are of 'low cost to you and high benefit to them and vice versa'. An example might be where the manufacturer of a line of crockery wants to sell their products into a specific retail chain which would be a big enough customer to allow them to launch the product. In this case, it may be that offering the chain an initial period of exclusivity will give them extra value that doesn't cost the manufacturer anything.

Fisher and Ury then suggest using 'objective criteria' as a test for any proposed solution to the problem. This has the advantage of focusing both parties on what would actually constitute an acceptable outcome and how they would measure that. Finally, but crucially, they tell the negotiator their BATNA (Best Alternative To Negotiated Agreement). This is a bedrock of negotiation – if we don't know from the start what our alternative is, given a failure to reach agreement, we can be forced into weak agreements because we haven't assessed whether no agreement would be a better option.

The great value of *Getting to Yes* is that it makes the reader fundamentally reassess their approach to negotiation. It is one of the handful of titles that I would wholeheartedly recommend to anyone in business, no matter what their personality or approach. The many specific examples given in the book give the reader a far deeper understanding of how they can use principled negotiation than any summary could. And while there have been many other books on negotiation before and after *Getting to Yes,* there are none that can match its clarity, brevity and value.

Getting to Yes

We all negotiate on a regular basis, in our personal lives as well as in business. It is essential for all negotiators to use principled negotiation and non-adversarial bargaining to look for mutual solutions to a problem rather than thinking of negotiation as a competition. With this aim, you can focus on the following five steps:

1. Separate the people from the problem.

2. Focus on interests, not positions.

3. Invent options for mutual gain.

4. Insist on using objective criteria.

5. Know your BATNA (Best Alternative To Negotiated Agreement).

The One Minute Manager

Ken Blanchard and
Spencer Johnson, 1982

Is it unreasonable to suggest that this book was the start of the rot? That its trite and vacuous but undeniably catchy approach was the inspiration for the hundreds of similarly useless books on management and business that have blighted the world in subsequent decades? Or that it is symptomatic of the decline of the publishing industry that a book that consists of a single crass idea could sell so many millions of copies when it probably shouldn't have been accepted for publication in the first place?

Since those are fairly strong charges, let's start by examining the evidence as fairly as possible. 'The One Minute Manager' is a title that promises to teach the reader simple tricks that will allow them to become a brilliant manager overnight and, even better, to be able to do so in one-minute chunks. If only life were really so simple.

The book takes the form of a fable in which a young manager goes on a quest to find the secrets of great management. Imagine a business-oriented version of *The Little Prince* but without an ounce of the wisdom, compassion and humour of that classic. The young manager meets the fabled One Minute Manager and learns by talking to him and his colleagues how he has become such a great leader, even though he only spends a few hours a week actually managing them.

The basic message of the book could be conveyed in a three-line postcard, which is presumably why the authors chose to use the fable form to drag it out a bit. The method described is: 1 – take some time to agree goals that can be summarised in 250 words for each employee; 2 – when you see them doing something good, praise them for one minute; 3 – when you see them doing something wrong, reprimand them for one minute.

You could describe dog training in similar terms and it would be similarly misleading – because, as important as it is to be honest in your criticisms in the workplace, giving positive and negative reinforcement the same weight is likely to backfire in practice. This kind of clumsiness suggests that the book has been written to a plan that was drawn up in isolation rather than as a result of the real-world experience that a writer like Peter Drucker (see p. 47) relied on. To a cynic, it might even imply that the authors are mere publishing hacks rather than having any actual experience of genius management in the workplace.

The advice on giving praise and criticism actually goes further down the rabbit hole, suggesting in both cases that the manager should make physical contact with the employee – a friendly hand on the shoulder or arm or similar. In the case of reprimands, the suggestion is that thirty seconds of clear criticism should be followed by the reassurance that the manager is only making this criticism for the good of the employee and that in other respects everything is fine. This is one of the creepiest bits of advice I have seen in a business book; in some situations it could easily lead to a sexual harassment case, but there are many other moments when it would come across as mildly demented. If the employee happened to be on the autistic spectrum it could even result in them bolting from the room or hitting out in sheer panic – and that could even be for the 'one minute of praise', let alone for the one-minute reprimand coupled to a moment of insincere bonding.

If you are a manager, do not take the advice in this book. Do not touch people in a creepy way while you are praising or admonishing them. Do not fall for the idea that you can be a great manager while solving all problems in sixty seconds. Many problems you will have to address will take considerably more consideration and effort.

There are a few fragments of common sense scattered among the nonsense. For instance, the authors are right to point out that managers need to constantly give employees feedback and not store up grievances and complaints for a specific assessment. But this is a really basic idea which you will find explained more clearly in other, far better guides to management.

It is also worth noting that there was a controversy about how much of this book might or might not have been plagiarised from an article by Arthur Elliott Carlisle, a professor at the University of Massachusetts. Various excuses and explanations have been given over the years for the similarities. Given how basic the message of the book is, it's hard to ignore how much the two overlap: the only part of Carlisle's ideas that don't have a strong parallel in *The One Minute Manager* is the most human, empathetic part in which he emphasises the importance of giving employees credit for their ideas.

Ken Blanchard and Spencer Johnson went on to churn out many other books on management and other subjects, including (in the case of Johnson) the execrable *Who Moved My Cheese?* (see p. 115) which achieved the almost unthinkable feat of being even more fatuous than *The One Minute Manager.* And publishers around the world saw the success of these books and became all too eager to publish business books that involved stretching out a simple, inane concept that seemed too good to be true (and almost certainly was) and which almost certainly helped to lower management performance levels whenever such ideas were taken seriously. The only thing worse than a bad manager is a bad manager who has read a bad book about how to be a brilliant manager.

(OK, perhaps that wasn't the fairest summary of the evidence – but, trust me, if you make the mistake of reading this book yourself, you will come out of it wanting to see someone harshly punished for the hours of your life that you have wasted and which you will never get back.)

THE SPEED READ

The One Minute Manager

Somewhere in the world there is a godlike individual called the One Minute Manager* who makes the art of management look incredibly simple – in just a few hours a week, he achieves amazing things and all he ever needs to do to solve a problem is to ask employees to commit to goals (in 250 words) and then give them sixty seconds of praise or blame as and when they deserve it, while touching them in a deeply creepy and insincere way. The rest of the time he can sit in a hammock drinking cocktails or playing golf or driving an expensive car to a fancy holiday resort.

* This person does not exist. Do not read this book. And if you do accidentally read it, do not believe a word of it. Management is hard work and it takes a lot more than a minute here and there to make a business function well and to help employees to fulfil their potential.

In Search of Excellence

Lessons from America's Best-Run Companies

Robert H. Waterman Jr and
Tom Peters, 1982

Tom Peters and Robert H. Waterman Jr were management consultants with McKinsey & Company and this
book builds on research by the management consultancy
firm in the late 1970s. It then focused on the nature of the
relationship between strategy, structure and management
effectiveness. The study resulted in their now well-known
7-S framework of management effectiveness (structure,
strategy, systems, shared values, skills, style and staff). The
authors wanted to build on this by looking at management
excellence itself and in this book lay out eight key attributes
that they see as standing out in excellent, innovative companies. The result was one of the best-selling business books
of all time, which devotes a chapter to each of the eight
themes that the authors see as common characteristics of
successful companies.

The first is a 'bias for action', which relies on active decision-making. Enabling quick decisions avoids unnecessary
bureaucratic control. For Waterman and Peters, this involves

open communication between employees and management and makes the company more open to experimentation. The second factor is being 'close to the customer', which requires reliability, a good service ethos and the ability to gain and retain customers. The authors argue that this is achieved by learning from the people the company wants to serve.

'Autonomy and entrepreneurship' is the third key element, which necessitates the encouragement of creativity by allowing for in-house competition at employee level. This fosters and nurtures innovation and keeps the company at the top of its game. Fourth is 'productivity through people', which involves looking at all employees, at whatever level, as a source of quality. The idea is that treating your workforce with respect makes them feel valued and this increases productivity.

The fifth theme is that management should be hands-on and value-driven. In this way, the authors argue, management can show their commitment to the company and the staff. The sixth chapter has the wacky title 'Stick to the knitting', which is just a reference to the idea that it is better to stay with the business you know, to understand what the company's primary business is and not to diversify into areas where there is no expertise. The seventh common element is to have a simple structure and lean staff. The authors argue against excessively complex management structures, preferring to maximise a company's ability to implement any necessary changes quickly. This makes the company more adaptable and sustainable in the face of market changes. Finally the authors address balance, in the chapter 'Simultaneous loose-tight properties', which also sums up and gives an overview of the previous seven themes. They argue that there must be a balance of central direction and individual autonomy. The company should have a definite focus, but within that there should be room for individual innovation. This combination of centralised values held by everyone with shop-floor autonomy results in better productivity which fosters success.

The eight principles still stand up as benchmarks for running a successful company but they will seem fairly obvious to anyone with genuine business experience or who has read any subsequent business books (many of which refer back to this classic either explicitly or implicitly). So while the authors make many excellent points and clearly know their subject, this doesn't feel like an especially inspirational read today.

The chapters are also padded out with reference to 'excellent' companies as examples. However, a number of these companies have been through significant difficulties in the interim, which slightly undermines the case the authors are making. And the book also feels rather dated – globalisation, increasing technological innovation and the aftermath of the crash of 2008 have perhaps made following these principles less of a guarantee of success than they once seemed.

THE SPEED READ

In Search of Excellence

A classic business title which analyses some common factors in successful companies.

Have a bias for getting things done, facilitate quick decision-making. Learn from your customers. Nurture innovation and encourage creative autonomy on the shop floor. Treat all employees as a source of quality – it will make them more productive. Value a hands-on management style and show commitment. Stay with what you know: don't diversify if there is no expertise in that area within the company. Have a minimal management team: it stops the company becoming too bureaucratic and stagnating. Keep sight of the common values of the company but allow as much autonomy as possible on the shop floor.

Guerrilla Marketing

Jay Conrad Levinson, 1984

When *Guerrilla Marketing* was first published in 1984 it defined a radical new way of approaching business. The fact that the techniques of marketing that it outlined have now become utterly mainstream does not mean that this book is obsolete. On the contrary, it remains a valuable introduction to the subject of marketing, especially for those who want to achieve extraordinary results on a limited budget.

From the outset, Jay Conrad Levinson makes many valuable points in succinct and memorable ways. For instance, he defines marketing as 'every bit of contact your company has with anyone in the outside world. Every bit of contact.' He also insists that you should see marketing as a long-term commitment, a marathon rather than a sprint. He constantly emphasises the importance of winning trust from consumers, pointing out that it might be the fifth, tenth or twentieth time you contact a lead that actually results in sales, so you need a strategy that can allow for that longevity.

Levinson was prescient in his understanding of how the internet and new media would shape marketing and added useful material on this subject to later editions but, unlike many early adopters, he didn't make the mistake of confusing internet traffic with successful business. He argues that marketing should be measured by profits and sales, not by hits or page impressions. Even today, this message is too often neglected by marketing departments who will circulate weekly round-ups of how many new followers they have, how many views they have had on social media and so on, when the crucial question is, 'But did this drive any actual sales?' A classic mistake that is made in publishing businesses is, for instance, to say, 'This writer has 10,000 followers on Tweeble, Fitbook, or Instagrin, so therefore we will make at least 1,000 sales to those people,' when the actual figures can be closer to one sale per 100,000 followers – unless you target your marketing precisely.

While the book was reworked several times, most recently in 2007, you do have to be aware that some of the specific advice in *Guerrilla Marketing* is dated. Consumers have become ever more sophisticated in their understanding of how messages are targeted at them and, to take one example, they would no longer be impressed by being added to an email group after a casual business encounter. But given the proviso that particular suggestions should be treated cautiously, it is well worth reading for broader inspiration and ideas.

And some of the specific advice is still as relevant as it was in 1984. For instance, Levinson's summary of how to write a 'seven-sentence marketing plan' has rarely been bettered. Briefly, this involves a sentence setting out your objective (and this must be something that can be monitored, ideally in terms of actual sales or profits, but at least in terms of measurable results), followed by a sentence on the specific competitive advantage you want to emphasise, then one sentence on your target audience (which should be as detailed as possible

– Levinson always stresses that focusing strong marketing on a modest number of actual customers or well targeted leads is many times more effective than a slingshot approach). The fourth sentence is actually a list of the marketing tools you are planning to use – and Levinson has a bewildering array of options, some obvious, some wildly inventive. Finally, add sentences describing your niche in the marketplace, your identity as a company and the marketing budget, expressed as a percentage of your gross sales. Following Levinson's suggested approach you really can write a useful marketing overview in five to ten minutes.

As an experienced advertising guru, Levinson has a lot of basic practical advice – for instance, he suggests that half of your marketing energy should be devoted to existing customers and emphasises the importance of visual communication and of talking directly to the customer through 'you' marketing. He describes marketing as a conversation between the company and the consumer, a concept that may seem obvious now, but that was less so in 1984 when a large proportion of marketing still went through traditional channels. In this conversation, you need to inspire trust in the customer and this has to be a holistic part of the way that your company does business, meaning that the concept of customer service becomes much more central to how your company projects its image and identity into the world.

Levinson argues that, whatever business you think you are in, you are actually in at least three other businesses at the same time: the marketing business, which you need to be aware of at all times; the service business, through which you win the trust and belief of your customers; and the 'people business', given that your ability to motivate and persuade people depends on your genuine interest in them.

Another idea that Levinson champions is that small businesses should look around them in the marketplace and find ways to practice 'fusion marketing', meaning that they collaborate with other businesses in ways that will bring them mutual marketing advantages.

At times in the book he is bombastic and at times he is wrong (for instance, in his casual dismissal of the importance of internet sales of printed books). In the 2007 edition of the book he rather complacently observes that his book, which was once radical, is now on so many business courses as a set text that it has become mainstream. You need to treat him as you would a loquacious friend who occasionally gets things bizarrely wrong, but who usually talks solid common sense and is therefore always worth talking to.

Later editions can also be infuriating for the degree to which they direct the reader to the many other titles in the *Guerrilla Marketing* franchise: Levinson was an advocate of cross-selling, but the degree to which he indulges in it in his own books actually demonstrates how counterproductive and irritating this approach can be. But for all its faults, this remains a book that can inspire any business person to think of inventive, budget-conscious ways of improving their marketing skills.

┌─ THE SPEED READ ─────────────────────

Guerrilla Marketing

Marketing is a long-term commitment, in which every bit of contact your company has with potential customers matters, from first impressions to sale through to service. In the modern world (whether that be in 1984 or the twenty-first century), traditional marketing has been partially displaced by 'guerrilla marketing', in which small companies can make a huge impact using low-cost, creative methods. Measure your marketing in concrete terms, for instance by the sales and profits it generates, not how much attention it gets. Focus half your marketing on existing customers, because marketing is not just about getting people to change their minds, it is also about persuading them to maintain their mindset if they are already inclined to do business with you. You can outsource many of the specific tasks involved in marketing, but in the end you are the person who truly understands your products, so the creative spark in your guerrilla marketing must always come from you.

The Art of the Deal

Donald Trump and Tony Schwartz, 1987

The Art of the Deal was Donald Trump's first book. Never one to suffer from false modesty, he has hailed it as his second-favourite book after the Bible and the best-selling business book of all time. As with so many statements about the forty-fifth President of the United States of America, the latter claim is questionable, although it may just sneak into the Top 10. Even the authorship of the book is disputed – Tony Schwartz was brought in to write the book by the publisher and spent time with Trump, recording his words and interpreting them, but each claims the other had very little to do with the book and Trump has threatened to take Schwartz to court for his royalties. (Schwartz now publicly repudiates the book, expressing the view that if he rewrote it now, he would call it *The Sociopath*.)[1]

So far, so predictably murky. But is it a good book, or even an enjoyable one? The first thing to note is that the formula for success described in the book is a pretty hackneyed one, which relies heavily on 'thinking big', 'knowing your market'

---

[1] Jane Mayer, 'Donald Trump's Ghostwriter Tells All' in *The New Yorker*, 25 July 2016

and other similar cliches. In this respect the book says little that hasn't been said better in books like *The Power of Positive Thinking* and *How to Win Friends and Influence People* (or expressed in a similarly infuriating fashion in *Think and Grow Rich,* which may have indirectly influenced Trump's thinking).

Whether you find the book enjoyable or not will depend 'bigly' on how you feel about Trump. If you see him as a titan of industry and an acceptable president, or can at least find his braggadocio tolerable, then his narcissistic character is caught well by this book, much of which is taken up with his musings on his own successes and virtues. However, if you find him appalling and a symbol of everything that is going wrong in the world, you will also find plenty of material here to support your gut feeling.

The book is surprisingly honest about some of Trump's early battles with zoning authorities, banks and other obstacles that lay in his path as he traversed the tricky route from millionaire to billionaire (the latter claim being subject to revision if we ever get chapter and verse on Trump's finances – at the time of writing he has released a financial disclosure form but his tax returns remain stubbornly stuck down the back of his sofa). As a result, the book doesn't truly instruct readers on how to make deals, as it is heavily dependent on suggesting you can get your way by sheer force of personality.

However, there are some interesting lessons that can be taken from the book, if you are willing to give Trump a pass on his more problematic features. Firstly, you do get a sense of his close attention to detail, from his obsessive interest in the fittings in Trump Tower to the way he micromanages subcontractors and his staff. His sharp focus on every stage of the process is reminiscent of many other entrepreneurs who have built up businesses. Rather than assuming he can leave the small stuff to employees, he turns up for every planning meeting and shouts and stamps his feet if he feels he is not getting a good enough level of work and attention.

This is an approach to business that won't suit everyone but may be invaluable for those who want to build up a business from scratch and who want to have a visceral understanding of every single element of that business from the nuts and bolts that hold it together, to the details of payroll, the office furniture and the accounting systems. And while Trump can come across as penny-pinching (and has, among many other complaints, been heavily criticised over the details of some of his business transactions on that basis), it can't be denied that he knows how to control costs, which is one of the key elements of any business.

As the original inspiration for the ghastly Biff Tannen in *Back to the Future*, Trump is easy to mock. Although, as I write (two days after the 2016 US presidential election) it seems that he has had the last laugh, which is a weird vindication of some of his adages in *The Art of the Deal*, from 'thinking big' onwards. It remains to be seen how his rather bombastic approach to business translates into the political realm.

Either way, this is a book that can be enjoyed for a variety of reasons: not the least of which is that it is more inadvertently revealing of the real Trump than some of his later books. At the very least it paints a portrait of the sort of man who can build Trump Tower and the associated business empire and can muscle his way to the White House by sheer force of will.

The Art of the Deal

My name is Donald Trump and I don't take 'No' for an answer. If you're going to waste time thinking about stuff, you might as well think big and, if you think big, you are going to win big. (Especially if you start out with a loan of a few million from your daddy.) You might even want to think bigly, if you want to end up winning bigly. And if you haven't realised the power of thinking big and not taking 'No' for an answer yet, then just think about this:

My name is President Donald Trump.

7 Habits of Highly Effective People

Powerful Lessons in Personal Change

Stephen Covey, 1989

If you want to know how to become a better person, then you should look at your role models and try to emulate their behaviour. On the face of it, that sounds like a reasonable statement, the starting point for *7 Habits of Highly Effective People*. This was a hugely successful book on leadership and personal development.

Covey believed that self-improvement literature in America had changed over time – until the period between the two world wars, it had mostly focused on what he called the 'character ethic', meaning it focused on qualities such as integrity, honesty and courage and the ways these helped people to live good lives. Through the twentieth century, he felt that the focus had shifted to the 'personality ethic', in which readers were given quick fixes and ways to present and sell themselves to the world, rather than ways to make genuine spiritual progress (Covey was a member of the Church of Jesus Christ of Latter-day Saints, more commonly known as the Mormons, and his Christian beliefs strongly inform his writings.)

In an attempt to counter these more shallow tendencies, Covey distinguished between principles and values. He describes principles as timeless, objective and arising from the basic condition. For instance, the principle, 'If I don't tell the truth, I won't be trusted in future', is a fairly universal human truth. By contrast, he describes values as being more personal and subjective, although a person can make a timeless principle such as the Golden Rule ('Do unto others as you would have them do unto you') into a personal value. A person's values will dictate how they behave, but the consequences will ultimately be defined by principles.

Through a mixture of anecdotes and homely wisdom, Covey describes the way that a human moves from dependence (when, for instance, a child depends on its parents) to independence and he argues that the highest human achievements are a result of interdependence, in which humans work together towards common goals.

From these foundations, Covey lays out his seven habits, which he claims will help the reader to live a better, more confident and effective life if practised together. He describes these habits as 'the intersection of knowledge, skill and desire'.

At this point it should be mentioned that *7 Habits of Highly Effective People* is a book that really divides opinion, with some readers loving and others hating it. One test to reveal which camp you fall into is whether you regard the seven habits as profound and wise or irritatingly bland and obvious. Look away now if you don't like spoilers, but the habits are as follows:

- **Be proactive**
- **Begin with the end in mind**
- **Put first things first**
- **Think win/win**

- **Seek first to understand, then to be understood**
- **Synergise**
- **Sharpen the saw**

Most of these habits really are as obvious and self-explanatory as they look. The last ('Sharpen the saw') is just an admonition to make time for physical exercise, spiritual contemplation, worthy reading and so on. However, the apparent blandness of these habits when they are stated as baldly as above doesn't really do justice to the more interesting aspect of the book, which lies in the level detail.

To take an example, the third habit is to put first things first. So far, so obvious. But when it comes to explaining this habit, Covey makes some valuable points. Firstly, he points out that while you can be *efficient* with things, you need to be *effective* with people. In other words, relationships take time and can't be rushed for the sake of efficiency. And people are more important than things, so you need to plan your time accordingly. (Note how refreshing this viewpoint is when juxtaposed with the maxims of the *The One Minute Manager*, which argues that a manager can deal with employees in hyper-efficient, sixty-second bursts).

He also distinguishes between urgent tasks and important tasks – one of the more useful tools he describes in the book is a simple 2 x 2 matrix into which you can sort the tasks and other claims on your attention in the average working week. On one axis you sort tasks into 'urgent' and 'not urgent', while in the other you separate them into 'important' and 'not important'. Many tasks that are 'urgent' – preparing for a meeting which won't actually achieve a great deal or responding to emails you have been copied into – turn out to be 'not important'. Conversely, there are tasks – such as planning for the future – which may never become 'urgent' but which are always 'important'. This is a really useful exercise for focusing your mind on which activities are worthwhile and which you should be attempting to minimise.

So there are genuinely interesting moments in this book. However, it is a long and dense read and there are also valid criticisms that can be made. For instance, Covey talks of 'correct principles' and appeals to the 'natural law' that is common across Judaeo-Christian thought and all major religions. This is philosophically woolly at best and is too often allied to an interpretation of principles that feels rooted in a specific time and place. And Covey is prone to using pompous pieces of pseudo-widsom that seem appealing on first sight, but collapse into meaninglessness the more you think about them. He writes, for instance, 'It's not what happens to us, but our response to what happens to us, that hurts us,' which would be pretty useless advice to the victim of a car crash, for one. Elsewhere, he comes out with barely comprehensible phrases such as, 'What you are shouts so loudly in my ears I cannot hear what you say.' This tendency to vacuous sermonising is the weakest aspect of the book.

In the end, this isn't really a book about business or leadership. It is a book about spirituality. From that point of view it is an interesting read that will strike more of a chord with some readers than others. Given that it has sold more than twenty-five million copies and has many fervent fans, the best advice might be to give it a try and see how you react to the first fifty pages. If at this point you are finding it a profound insight into life, you will probably want to continue reading. If you just find it infuriating, then you're highly unlikely to have your mind changed by going on to read the rest of the book.

┌─ **THE SPEED READ** ─────────────────────────────┐

7 Habits of Highly Effective People

Self-improvement used to focus on the 'character ethic' but in the second half of the twentieth century it focused on the 'personality ethic', which was basically about pretending to become a better person rather than really becoming one. There are timeless principles that can help build character if you adopt some of them as your personal values. In life, humans move on from dependence to independence – but the highest stage of progress is interdependence. In order to make progress, you should adopt some habits that will help to unite your knowledge and skills with timeless principles of human behaviour. A very brief summary of these habits would be: don't procrastinate, plan ahead, focus on important stuff, be co-operative, be empathetic, synergise (whatever that means) and make time in your life for exercise, meditation and reading. On first reading, this advice may sound shallow and inane – whether you find the book worthwhile in spite of this will depend on how you connect to the author, whose detailed discussion of these basic habits is rarely less than provocative and interesting.

└──┘

Barbarians at the Gate

The Fall of RJR Nabisco

Bryan Burrough and John Helyar, 1989

The excesses of Wall Street in the 1980s were captured well in the media, including the movie *Wall Street* (1987) and *Liar's Poker*, Michael Lewis's 1989 book in which he described his own experiences as a rookie in the financial district. He tells the story of some of the characters who came to define the era, including Lewis Ranieri, who was in charge of the Salomon Brothers mortgage bond trading desk through its spectacular rise and fall and Michael Milken, the junk bond king. We'll look at the more recent Michael Lewis book, *The Big Short*, later. But for a really forensic examination of what was going wrong in the 1980s, one of the best places to start is *Barbarians at the Gate*.

Burrough and Helyar were investigative journalists from the *Wall Street Journal* who were separately covering the story of the 1988 buyout of RJR Nabisco, the American food and tobacco conglomerate. At the time this was the biggest leveraged buyout in history and a huge news story which was regarded by many as the epitome of corporate excess and an indictment of the greed of executives. The publisher Harper & Row invited the two to collaborate on a book and *Barbarians at the Gate* was the result.

It tells a tangled story. F. Ross Johnson, the CEO of the company, had discussed the buyout with Henry Kravis and George R. Roberts of Kohlberg Kravis Roberts and Co., a multi-national private equity company that had made a speciality of leveraged buyouts. In the end, Johnson chose to pursue an alternative route to the management buyout, working with an equity division of American Express. A fearsome bidding battle ensued, with the sums involved exceeding £25 billion. Most of the major private equity firms, including Goldman Sachs, Forstmann Little and Morgan Stanley, also became involved in the battle.

KKR ultimately won the battle in spite of a higher bid from F. Ross Johnson's alliance with American Express. There were two reasons for this: firstly, the board of directors had foreseen the apparently higher bid might end up being worth less due to the complications of the deal and, secondly, there were some serious concerns about the level of remuneration that Johnson himself would have received as a result of the deal going through: he stood to personally make up to $100 million. In December 1988, *Time* Magazine featured Johnson on the cover with the title THE GAME OF GREED accompanying an article questioning whether the buyout craze had gone too far.

The authors give a dry and meticulous but nonetheless hilarious account of the skirmishes in this battle and of the monstrous egos and manoeuvring of many of the participants. The kinds of characters that Michael Lewis would describe as the 'Big swinging dicks of Wall Street'[1] are captured here in all their macho pomp, with an even clearer understanding by the authors of the dangers that such personalities posed.

---

[1] Michael Lewis, *Liar's Poker* (1989), W.W. Norton & Company, New York, 2010, p.56

The outcome of the RJR Nabisco buyout was a huge amount of debt being transferred onto the company and the sell-off of numerous divisions to other corporations.

The leveraged buyout is a peculiar twentieth-century invention in which private equity players are allowed to purchase companies with extraordinary amounts of debt. The evidence over the years has been that this usually benefits the banks and the financial corporations, but rarely makes the company into a stronger business in the medium to long term. The title *Barbarians at the Gate* comes from Ted Forstmann of Forstmann Little who, according to Heylar and Burrough, described the KKR buyout money as 'phoney junk bond crap' in contrast to the real people with real money he saw his own firm as epitomising. He went on to argue that people like KKR were corporate raiders whose activities meant 'We need to push the barbarians back from the city gates.'

Of course history tells us that the barbarians were never really pushed back and that, after some brief interludes, leveraged buyouts and other questionable business practises have continued to wreak havoc. Books such as *Barbarians at the Gate* and *Liar's Poker* could (and probably should) have been taken as cautionary tales, but often had the opposite effect – Lewis mentioned in the introduction to *The Big Short* that he hoped that his first book would put bright people off from wasting their time in Wall Street, but instead he found himself deluged by messages asking for his advice on how to break into that world.

Interviewed recently, Helyar and Burrough said they regretted the degree to which Wall Street has moved on from 'real money'. Helyar pointed out that when they wrote the book, 'M&A artists were over-the-top in some cases but were still tethered to real corporate America.' He compared this to the 'blue smoke and mirrors environment' of Wall Street today as quants and corporate raiders find ever more arcane ways to exploit the way that deals are made in the financial markets.[2]

While some of the details of what went on in Wall Street in the 1980s may now seem quaint and mild compared to the later madness and devastation revealed by the global financial crisis, *Barbarians at the Gate* is one of the best places to start if you want to understand how greed, fear, pride and irrationality feed into deals such as leveraged buyouts, and how good companies can be ruined by the machinations of the financial sector.

THE SPEED READ

Barbarians at the Gate

The story of the leveraged buyout of RJR Nabisco in 1988, told by two investigative journalists who covered the story for the *Wall Street Journal*. One of the books that defined the hedonism, greed and macho irrationality of Wall Street in the 1980s, this can be read as a cautionary tale of what can go wrong within a business when the stakes are high and managers can seek excessive rewards. It is also a primer for the way the financial sector started to run amok, using mergers and acquisitions and other deals to generate huge profits for a few, to the detriment of many ordinary workers and citizens. It is widely regarded as one of the best business books of all time.

---

[2] Jon Friedman, '"Barbarians At The Gate": Authors Reflect On Wall Street's Madness' on *CBS MoneyWatch*, 21 November 2008

The E-Myth Revisted

Why Most Small Businesses Don't Work and What to Do About It

Michael E. Gerber, 1995

Michael E. Gerber is a small business consultant and in this revised version of his well-known 1986 book, *The E-Myth*, he gives a step-by-step approach to building a successful small business. The E-Myth (or Entrepreneurial Myth) is, for Gerber, the myth that businesses are started by entrepreneurs looking to make a profit. Instead, he argues, most small businesses are actually run by 'technicians' (employees) and they fail because the technician knows about the product but doesn't understand the nature of the business itself.

Instead of the technician alone, Gerber argues, a successful business needs three personalities to make it work: the Entrepreneur – the dreamer who sets out to do something new; the Technician – an expert in his or her craft; and the Manager – detail-orientated and able to organise. According to the author, we all have these three personalities inside us. It's just a matter of putting them together and operating in the right way.

The bulk of the book is a compilation of many systems and strategies that a small-business developer must apparently follow to be successful. Gerber argues that to be successful, your business must be able to operate without you and for this you need a system. Gerber calls this the Franchise Prototype, getting inspiration from chains such as McDonalds and Subway where there are manuals that describe in detail how to run the business so that it can be operated all over the world with continuity. This means employing staff that understand exactly how the business operates – people able to follow your instructions according to the system you have devised. Gerber insists that operating manuals are crucial and that you should know exactly how you want your business to operate.

Once you have your business model and manuals you need to keep up the momentum through Innovation (using creativity to improve your business), Quantification (measuring how successful each innovative idea is) and Orchestration (standardising what works so that every employee understands and can operate it). Presumably the orchestration involves yet more work on the manual. Along the way, there are bizarre suggestions about uniforms, standardisation and codes that make it sound as if you will be setting up a battery farm rather than creating a business.

Perhaps it is the constant references to fast-food outlets (and franchises) that make this book feel repetitive and narrow. There has been so much discussion in the media over the years about what it's like to work for these companies that one can't help feeling a little depressed by the extreme level of control Gerber advocates and that he expects you to reproduce on paper.

He also argues that you should have a Primary Aim in your life that isn't business-related so that your business won't consume you. This means that your business should be a route to your primary aim and not the end in itself.

This is a guide on how to have supreme control over a business when you're not actually there and inevitably this means creating lots of rules that must be followed in The Manual and involves a fair bit of jargon. There are the strategies – apparently you need a Management Strategy (having systems in place), a People Strategy (making sure you have employees who understand and can follow the rules) and a Marketing Strategy (learning your key demographic and looking at how others market to that demographic). Then there are the Systems: Hard (tools of the trade to make things easier), Soft (practices and methods for employees to follow) and Information (information and data gathering). And, according to Gerber, all of these together define the route your business must follow.

There isn't much room for excitement or innovation here. Probably because the franchise chains used as examples are not unique or innovative but mundane and uniform. Still, they work and have earned their founders a fortune so, depending on your aspirations, Gerber's advice might just be useful to you. If you like to wear a uniform . . .

THE SPEED READ

The E-Myth Revisited

You must fulfil three roles to run a successful business: the Technician, the Manager and the Entrepreneur. Follow the Franchise Prototype – your business must be able to operate without you. Create The Manual and keep adding to it – make sure anyone can understand and implement it. Your business should complement your Primary Aim in life. You need Systems – write them down! You need Strategies – write them down! Consider uniforms for staff, uniform business practices and uniform premises. Now, go sit under a palm tree, while occasionally checking that everyone is following your rules.

Emotional Intelligence

Why It Can Matter More Than IQ

Daniel Goleman, 1995

This is undoubtedly an important and influential book. It transformed the way that people talk about the whole concept of intelligence and has had a huge impact on the way that children are educated and the ways that companies evaluate employees. As to the question of whether or not it is a good book, let's reserve judgement for a few moments.

Daniel Goleman, who was working as a science reporter for the *New York Times,* was inspired by an academic article by John Mayer and Peter Salovey, in which they wrote about 'emotional intelligence'.[1] This was in itself an idea that had been mentioned in psychological articles as far back as 1964, but they gave it a particularly clear articulation. They described it as a different kind of intelligence to IQ, which dominated discussions of personality and aptitude at the time, and broke it down into subcategories: perceiving emotions, reasoning with emotions, understanding emotions and managing emotions.

---

[1] Mayer, J.D. and Salovey, P. (1990) 'Emotional Intelligence' in *Imagination, Cognition and Personality*, 9, 185-211.

Goleman's 1995 book was the first written for a popular audience on the subject, although he did take care to ground the discussion in as much scientific research as possible. He started by noting the crucial role that emotions played in human evolution, writing, for instance, 'Fear, in evolution, has a special prominence: perhaps more than any other emotion it is crucial for survival.' He also noted how emotions such as love and craving drove our primal instincts and were rooted in the 'limbic system'.

Goleman views rationality as a construct that is laid on top of these primal emotions and the great challenge facing humans in the modern world is how to understand, recognise and channel these emotions in a useful way. This is the core of his idea of emotional intelligence, the idea that dealing intelligently with our emotions and those of other people is crucial to our success and competence in life.

He focused in particular on how emotional intelligence feeds into leadership skills and gave his own analysis of its components, breaking it down into self-awareness, self-regulation, social skill, empathy and motivation. Within each of these areas, he identified a range of emotional competencies – skills that can be learned. An individual may be born with more or less emotional intelligence, but they can improve their emotional competencies through practice.

Part of Goleman's thesis is that people who have well-developed social and emotional skills are less prone to being overwhelmed by their emotions and more able to channel them. This makes them more effective in the workplace and better at understanding and motivating those around them. People who fail to properly identify and control their emotions are in a constant struggle that detracts from their ability to focus and concentrate on the important tasks facing them.

Thus far, it is hard to argue with Goleman and it was a much-needed point that he was making. It is clearly true that leadership and business success do not depend on intelligence alone and the concept of emotional intelligence legitimised discussion of traits such as empathy, compassion and co-operation. It is arguable that it did this mainly by using a relatively dry academic term to refer to traits that had commonly been seen as 'feminine' or 'soft'. Talking in terms of emotional intelligence or EQ (emotional quotient) put such traits on a level with IQ in the eyes of business people, who have often taken a relatively macho or tough approach to evaluating people.

Where the book does start to come off the rails is in some of the more detailed analysis – it is a densely written book, to the point of being boring at times, but it also includes some unjustifiably bold claims. For instance, without substantiation he argues that across history great leaders have tended to be people with high EQ levels. He also makes some fairly wacky projections about future crime waves (due to insufficient EQ skills among the population) which have been proven false in the decades since the book was published.

The other problematic area is the legacy of his book. Companies and educators are now much more aware of the emotional aspects of intelligence and in some respects this is a positive thing. In particular, Goleman was proud of how many schools and colleges had taken his ideas on board – one example being the SEL (social and emotional learning) programmes run by Illinois schools. But there has been considerable academic criticism of Goleman's populist approach to the subject and considerable concerns raised about how accurately and how genuinely emotional intelligence can be measured. This is a particular concern as many employers have started to include emotional intelligence tests in their range of aptitude testing. And this concern becomes more serious when you take into account the fact that emotional intelligence testing will considerably disadvantage many people on the autism spectrum, who might nonetheless do a perfectly good job.

Then there is the concern that emotional intelligence is not the unalloyed virtue that Goleman suggests. Psychopaths can perform well on emotional intelligence tests, since they are good at identifying emotions in other people (if only because they want to be able to manipulate them). And Machiavellian behaviour in general can be more common and effective in people with high levels of emotional intelligence. Dr Martin Kilduff of University College London and his colleagues conducted an extensive review of the subject and pointed out that emotionally intelligent people 'intentionally shape their emotions to fabricate favorable impressions of themselves'.[2] For the most manipulative, ambitious people, then, it is extremely valuable to have an ability to understand and disguise their own emotions and to use their observations of other people's emotions to influence or undermine them.

So, coming back to the question of whether this is a good book, one can admit that it is an influential book that made an important point. But it is also a book that makes claims that are too strong to be supported by the evidence, that is frequently dull (and dated in parts), and that has had some unfortunate consequences. On the whole, it is still worth a read, but a pinch of salt is required.

---

[2] Martin Kilduff, Dan S. Ciabaru & Jochen I. Menges, 'Strategic use of emotional intelligence in organizational settings: Exploring the dark side' in *Research in Organisational Behaviour*, Volume 30, 2010, 129-152

Emotional Intelligence

As humans evolved, emotions (and the limbic system) played an important role in making us flee or fight when confronted with danger and to find ways to satisfy our drives. However, in the modern world, even the most intelligent of us can be overwhelmed by emotions that make it hard to be efficient and effective. The most successful managers and leaders have high emotional intelligence, meaning that they have a good understanding of their own emotions and those of other people, and a strong ability to control their own emotions while influencing other people by appealing to theirs. As a result, emotional intelligence can be more important than pure intelligence in the workplace and companies and educators should pay close attention to emotional intelligence when they assess capabilities and aptitudes.

Microserfs

Douglas Coupland, 1995

We haven't included many novels in this collection, for obvious reasons. But one aspect of business life that is sometimes captured best in fictional form is the experience of employees within a company.

Microserfs focuses on a group of geeks who are coding and testing for Microsoft and living on their campus. This story is set in the period before the release of the Windows 95 operating system, when the dot-com bubble was just starting to build, people still talked about the 'information superhighway' and geek culture hadn't yet taken over the world. Told in epistolary form, via Apple PowerBook entries, this is a mixture of sweetly comic misadventures and digressions in Coupland's trademark style (irritatingly tricksy or entertainingly post-modern, depending on your tastes).

It is as good a book as any at capturing the introspective obsessiveness of the tech industry. The characters attempt to divine the thoughts of the mighty Bill Gates, who is depicted as the feudal boss to their serfs. One character lives on a 'flatlander' diet, eating 'two-dimensional' food such as Kraft cheese slices that can be slid under doors, following a period in which he stays locked in his office (like many geeks and nerds he is on the autism spectrum).

The serfs bicker and exchange lists and cultural references (you need a good knowledge of 1970s' American TV culture to catch all of these) and ultimately strike out on their own to set up their own company, driven by fears over how short their careers in the corporation might be. Those who have been involved in tech start-ups will recognise the mixture of naivety, optimism and recklessness which drives this move, as well as the way that the normal practical issues that affect all businesses start to intrude into their lives.

The world in which these characters live is similar to recent TV series and films from *Office Space* to *The IT Crowd* and *The Big Bang Theory* to *Silicon Valley*. Like all of these, it is funniest and most absorbing for those with direct knowledge of the tech industry and geek culture, but accessible to anyone who has suffered the frustrations and minor insanities of the workplace. It is also a reminder to anyone who has read too many bombastic manuals on leadership and management that, ultimately, employees are all individuals who cannot for long be corralled into a company ethos that doesn't match up to their own worldview.

THE SPEED READ

Microserfs

A clever and funny novel in which mid-1990s techies are depicted as serfs within the machinery of the tech industry. A testament to geek culture that predates its current ubiquity and a reminder of how long ago the 1990s were and how different everything was before the dot-com bubble and the dawn of the twenty-first century.

The Dilbert Principle

Scott Adams, 1996

Business books tend to be aimed at either managers or those who aspire to rise through the ranks of the corporate world. They also tend to present a rather anodyne, sanitised version of the average workplace. So for a more honest, acerbic insight into what really goes on in offices and cubicles around the world, it's worth turning to Scott Adams, creator of the magnificent *Dilbert* cartoons.

The Dilbert Principle includes original comic strips by Adams, but it is also a prose guide to the more absurd corners of the corporate world, inspired by the many emails he received from readers of the strip, relating their own anecdotes of management idiocy and organisational chaos.

Adams is brilliant at skewering the more ridiculous management trends, the bureaucratic bear-traps of the human resources department, the infinite pain of pointless meetings and the horror of the performance review. Here he takes a look at topics such as business communication (which business-school professors believe to be about clarity and honesty and most executives see merely as a tool for career advancement), why mission statements are vacuous and

99

confused, and the importance of always looking busy at work (hint: always carry important-looking bits of paper).

The characters in *Dilbert* are mostly engineers in the tech industry but their daily battles are universal: who gets the best cubicle, why management makes so many absurd requests and the battle to befuddle fellow employees so that they are unsure whether you are a hard-working genius or merely idling along.

Adams ends up with some relatively serious suggestions as to how the workplace could be improved. One of these is for all office employees to go home at five o'clock on the basis that there are only so many hours in the day when anyone will be genuinely productive and that people with happy, balanced lives will on the whole do a better job.

The Dilbert Principle itself, which is at the core of the book, is a riposte to the Peter Principle (see p. 52). Instead of accepting Peter's theory that everyone rises to the level of their incompetence, Adams chooses to see the incompetence of management from a different point of view, arguing that organisations make a deliberate choice to put all of their most incompetent individuals in management positions in order to keep them out of harm's way. After all, if someone is a brilliant computer coder or a heart surgeon, you want them doing the actual work rather than filling in forms and attending meetings all day.

However, the unfortunate consequence of promoting all the idiots to management level is that they spend their time devising ways to create problems for everyone in the workplace and impeding the more competent individuals from simply getting on with what they are good at. So the Dilbert Principle becomes an albatross around the neck of organisations that end up being run incompetently as a result.

While this is a satirical take on the workplace, it will strike a chord with anyone who has had their time wasted by a boss who plainly doesn't understand the details of how his latest fad, system or reorganisation will actually affect the people who are doing all the work. As with the *Dilbert* strip in general, this may be uncomfortable reading for managers (especially any who are self-aware enough to suspect that deep down they really are the pointy-haired boss or Dogbert), but for most people with experience in a corporation, it will ring painfully and hilariously true.

THE SPEED READ

The Dilbert Principle

Based on the *Dilbert* cartoons and using its comic strips, this is Scott Adams' take on the workplace and a riposte to the Peter Principle. It argues that, rather than people naturally reaching the level at which they become incompetent, it is a necessary evil for companies and organisations to place their most useless individuals in supervisory or managerial roles, so that the competent individuals can do the real work that needs to be done. Painfully funny.

The Innovator's Dilemma
When New Technologies Cause Great Firms to Fail
Clayton M. Christensen, 1997

W hy is it that a good company can do everything the right way and nonetheless see their share of the market slipping away? Written by Harvard professor Clayton M. Christensen, *The Innovator's Dilemma* is a valuable attempt to explain how disruptive technologies and new products can transform an industry and why the biggest companies will often fail to generate such products.

The book takes an academic, detailed look at a variety of industries and products, from Intel's 8088 processor to the hydraulic excavator and IBM's Winchester disk drives, examining those points at which large, established companies have missed the next big wave. For instance, it discusses the way major motorbike manufacturers in the US lost market share to the Honda Super Cub, marketed as a friendly, modern, consumer appliance with the slogan 'You meet the nicest people on a Honda'. The Super Cub was bought by people who hadn't traditionally been bikers, such as young professionals – a demographic that had not been served well by traditional bikes with their appeal to a more macho, hard-nosed rider.

Christensen's general theory is based on two important observations. The first is that innovation follows an S-curve with respect to the value it delivers – at the start of a process of innovation, there is a lot of expense and dead ends and the value returned is low. Then, once the base is established, the product or technology is considerably enhanced by subsequent iterations of innovation and refinement. Finally, the market is fully established and further innovations deliver a declining return. At this point a company has achieved a significant market share: Christensen refers to such a company as an 'incumbent'. Incumbents have high sales expectations and an established customer base. If they 'do the right thing' and make sure they are meeting the expectations of their customer base and delivering product improvements based on research among that group, this automatically means that they are not looking for other niches for new-generation products. Smaller entrants to the market are motivated to look for those niches and, as they do not immediately require such high sales, they are able to build a product that appeals to different demographics and markets. As a result, the smaller company has an opportunity to create a new customer base which the larger company is failing to appeal to, since the larger company has to focus on sustaining technology rather than disruptive technology.

One of the historical examples that Christensen gives as evidence for this theory comes from the steel industry, which used to be dominated by large, integrated steel mills. When mini-mills were first established, they could only be used to make rebar, the lowest grade of steel. The customer base for this type of steel was a difficult market as it consisted of individuals and organisations looking for the cheapest possible solution to a problem. As a result, the integrated mills didn't see the mini-mills as serious competition and disregarded the low-value section of the market that they had lost. Over time the mini-mills went through a series of innovative improvements that allowed them to make better-quality steel and still the larger mills ignored the technology they were using. Finally, the mini-mills were able to match the quality of the integrated mills, but at lower cost and the integrated mills were driven out of business. The low-value parts of the market that they had felt able to ignore had gradually grown to encompass the entire market.

One objection that has been made to the book is that this is not an inevitable process. Some large companies continue to innovate and find new markets – Apple being an example of a company that might be expected to be usurped by disruptive technology based on Christensen's line of thinking. But, clearly, the process by which disruptive technologies can take over markets and industries is an important one to understand and this is a book which has important lessons for those working in incumbent companies. In the digital era it should be obvious how quickly market share can be wiped out by a new entry product.

When it comes to prescribing how companies can avoid falling prey to disruptive technologies, the book is perhaps less useful, but Christensen does make some suggestions. For instance, he advises companies to look beyond their current customer set to markets that may not exist yet and are thus hard to analyse, and he suggests setting up autonomous organisations whose sole purpose is to attempt to break into such new markets. These organisations should have access to the company's resources when needed but should have separate goals, processes and values. In these ways an incumbent company can find ways to allocate resources that overcome the systemic biases that arise from having a large, established customer base to service.

Christensen's point here could perhaps be made more simply with the old business saying, 'Never be afraid to compete with yourself.' These are wise words; if you don't do this, you can be sure that someone else will. Understanding the underlying biases that make it so hard for big companies to create disruptive products is a significant first step to overcoming those biases.

This book is mostly aimed at helping managers in large organisations as opposed to people who want to set up those smaller companies that create the innovations of the future. That said, there are lessons here for companies of any size, as the same dynamics that create problems for large companies create opportunities for new start-ups. At times Christensen's desire to ground the book in academic detail makes it a dry read, but this is undoubtedly an important book which forces the reader to think differently about how businesses can and should be run.

THE SPEED READ

The Innovator's Dilemma

An academic analysis of the underlying reasons why large, established companies can be usurped by smaller companies with new entry products. In particular, this book explains why a company with a strong customer base can do all the 'right things' by listening to their existing customers and reacting to their feedback, and, as a direct result, fail to see the niche opportunities for new product innovations which might appeal to demographics that they currently don't service. A book which is strongest when it is analysing the challenges faced by large companies, and weakest when it comes to suggesting solutions, its analysis is nonetheless groundbreaking and thought-provoking, whether you are part of an established company or pondering the dynamics which might allow a smaller start-up to take market share from the current incumbents.

The Essays of Warren Buffett

Lessons for Corporate America

Warren Buffett (with an introduction by Laurence Cunningham), 1998

Warren Buffett is an extremely canny investor and businessman whose thoughts are always worth reading. His annual letters to shareholders in Berkshire Hathaway, the hugely successful business of which he is CEO and the major shareholder, are a wonderful insight into the mind of a man who has acted with great integrity and common sense throughout his business career.

However, reading through the entirety of the letters can be time-consuming and repetitive and some of the matters he discussed in the older letters will be of no interest to today's reader. So a great place to start is by reading this collection which includes many extracts from those letters, arranged by subject matter with an introduction giving a useful overview of Buffett's thinking.

One of Buffett's core beliefs is that a CEO should treat his shareholders as he would want to be treated himself and these letters lay out clearly his principles and beliefs, in a style that is simple and direct (in keeping with his famously frugal lifestyle) and often charmingly funny to read. He is a strong advocate of full and fair reporting by CEOs and, refreshingly, suggests that CEOs should avoid predictions, because of the many unintended ways in which these can distort behaviour in a company.

Buffett's favourite period to hold a stock for is 'for ever' and he frequently reiterates his belief that investing in a company should be treated as part-ownership, with the same sense of responsibility and care. He rejects the belief that efficient markets ensure that companies are correctly valued, preferring to refer back to his mentor Benjamin Graham's parable about 'Mr Market', an illustration of how irrational the swings in stock prices can be (see p. 38). As a result, he is sceptical about the use of 'beta', the measure of volatility in stocks that some investors rely on to guard against excessively variable stocks. His main aim as an investor is to identify good companies (by learning and understanding as much about that company as he possibly can), to acquire stock in them at good prices and to hold on to them for the long-term. Berkshire Hathaway often buys companies from owners who will continue to run the business themselves but whether he achieves this or other executives are brought in, Buffett looks to have good managers who he trusts to run the companies that he owns or part-owns.

Buffett is also sceptical about the idea that diversification can protect an investor, stressing that it is best to stick to buying in areas you personally understand. This is one of the reasons he was able to avoid losing money in the dot-com boom, because he was reluctant to invest in businesses whose function he didn't get. And sticking to the fundamentals of what makes a good business was also the principle that allowed him to see that the 1980s' and 1990s' boom in junk bonds and zero-coupon bonds led to these assets being significantly overvalued. He writes well about the problems of mergers and acquisitions, wryly noting how often these have damaged the stock value of the company doing the takeover.

As part of his commitment to full and fair accounting, Buffett devotes considerable space to the problems of corporate reporting. He complains that the pressure to show significant profits and to meet targets, together with a mistaken focus on pushing the stock price up (as opposed to allowing it to reflect the true value of a company) have led to distortions and manipulations in the ways that companies report their finances. For instance, stock options are often not counted as a cost and retained earnings can be reported in an unclear manner.

Buffett is a follower of Graham in believing that it is important to observe how well companies invest retained earnings, arguing that if they can make better use of that cash than the stockholders then it makes sense for them not to pay a dividend if they have used the money wisely (and this will be reflected in the value of the stock). In pursuit of clarity on these issues, Buffett argues for the use of 'look-through earnings' in which retained earnings and dividends are clearly accounted for.

Unlike some business people, Buffett is happy to talk about his mistakes and what he has learned from them. One instance is his original purchase of Berkshire Hathaway, then a textiles firm that he believed he was buying for a good price but which he was eventually forced to close as the US textiles industry declined. He also defends and explains decisions that other people have criticised, one example being the long period for which he refused to do a stock split in his own company (followed by the issue of 'B shares' as an alternative approach).

There have been four editions of the book, at the time of writing, with the most recent adding material on the global financial crisis and the housing bubble that helped to provoke it, on the current state of financial reporting and on developing investment opportunities.

This book isn't a blueprint for how to make money like Warren Buffett, nor will it tell you the nuts and bolts of how to set up a small business. But it is a valuable insight into the mindset of a man who proves that in spite of the stereotypical corrupt bankers and the vulture capitalists, it is possible to be a successful investor while continuing to act with wisdom and decency.

THE SPEED READ

The Essays of Warren Buffett

A compressed primer of the ideas and values of one of the world's richest men, with extracts from his letters to the shareholders in Berkshire Hathaway. Here you can find Warren Buffett's thoughts on how to recognise a good business being run well and whether its stock is correctly valued or not. He also discusses corporate governance and financial reporting and airs his frustrations with poorly run businesses, CEOs who evade responsibility for their performance and companies that make ill-advised mergers and acquisitions, among many other topics. A clearly written, drily humorous guide to the world of investment from one of the very best, which both emphasises and embodies the value of full, clear and honest communication.

The 48 Laws of Power

Robert Greene, 1998

The story of how *The 48 Laws of Power* came to be published should perhaps be treated like a morality tale from which different readers may draw different conclusions . . .

Robert Greene was a middle-class Californian with liberal views who spent years trying to succeed as a writer. He worked as a screenwriter in Hollywood, where he noted with distaste the devious, immoral ways in which some of the movie executives attempted to manipulate and exploit him. He toyed with the idea of a kind of anti-self-help book which, rather than taking the sentimental 'you-can-do-it-if-you-believe-in-yourself' approach, acted like a manual for the sorts of people who had been messing him around.

Subsequently, he met the book packager Joost Elffers and suggested this idea to him. If you are not familiar with packager companies, they are a curious subsection of the publishing industry – they don't actually publish the books they create, but instead put together a proposal and attempt to sell it to multiple publishers around the world. It is a low-risk strategy as they needn't progress the books that don't sell and are guaranteed a profit on the ones that do. The downside is that ordinary publishers are somewhat snobbish about them (even the ones who frequently buy their titles) and the books themselves tend to be beautifully designed but somewhat banal, as they have to work in as many different territories as possible.

Any book publisher knows that one of the easiest types of books to make is one that compiles or reworks a selection of out-of-copyright material. But these days such books are harder to sell without a gimmick. In the case of *The 48 Laws of Power*, the packager put together a beautifully designed package, while Greene supplied a cynical but cleverly written summary of the 'laws' – essentially distillations of morals taken from the most ruthless leaders and powermongers of the past, from Machiavelli to Julius Caesar.

The resulting book has been called a 'psychopath's bible' because it advises the reader to (for instance) find each employee's 'thumbscrew', to get others to do the work while you take the credit, and to pose a friend while working as a spy. That's not even to mention Law 7, which tells you to 'avoid the unhappy and the unlucky'. Anyone who has been in a toxic workplace will recognise that there are indeed individuals who use such tactics on a daily basis, so one can acknowledge that, in spite of Greene's somewhat satirical intent, he depicts the thought processes of some people depressingly accurately.

Critics were not kind to the book, pointing out that its claims to be based on extensive historical knowledge were a bit shaky and that many of the laws contradict each other. For instance, you are told in Law 15 to crush your enemies completely, while Law 2 advises you to employ former enemies. Law 6 tells you to seek attention at all times whereas, later in the book, you are advised to act like those around you. One can perhaps excuse some of these contradictions on the basis of an *I Ching*-style duality of thought, but they do somewhat undermine the authority of the book.

In spite of its complicated origins, the book was a huge success, with the *Los Angeles Times* noting that it had made Greene a 'cult hero with the hip-hop set, Hollywood elite and prison inmates alike'.[1] Yes, as well as the book being a frequently requested book in prison libraries, it can count actor and musician Will Smith as a fan, while producers and rappers from Jay-Z to Calvin Harris have referred to the book and 50 Cent even co-wrote a follow-up, *The 50th Law*, with Greene.

To be fair, Greene is also proud that readers say the book has helped them to deal with the sociopathic behaviour of those around them in the workplace, and to finally understand and counteract the weaselling and manoeuvring of their work colleagues and bosses. So the book has its virtues whether you are aiming to act like a psychopath yourself or to defend yourself from one. And Greene's 2012 book, *Mastery*, is a much more thoughtful approach to the issue of power that acknowledges many of these issues.

So what moral should we take from the story? That there are more psychopaths in the world of business than we would like to think? That horrible behaviour will be rewarded? Or that publishing is a deeply cynical business?

Perhaps instead of passing judgement, we should take the advice of Greene's Law 4 and 'Always say less than necessary'.

---

[1] Andrea Chang, 'American Apparel's in-house guru shows a lighter side' in *Los Angeles Times*, 20 August 2011

The 48 Laws of Power

Psychopaths often win power and influence by being exploitative, dishonest and manipulative. So here is a manual on how to behave like one (or at least to understand their behaviour). Much of it is a rehash of *The Prince* by Machiavelli, although the author is also drawing on other historical sources as well as his own negative experience of the prima donnas and sociopaths of Hollywood who are now, curiously enough, among the book's biggest fans, along with prison inmates and gangsta rappers.

Who Moved My Cheese?

An Amazing Way to Deal with Change in Your Work and in Your Life

Dr Spencer Johnson, 1998

Sometimes a business can get a bit stuck in its ways and fail to adapt to the changing world.

This is a really basic concept. Indeed, it has just been fully explained in the single sentence above. But somehow *Who Moved My Cheese?* manages to translate this single sentence into a confusing parable about a group of mice and little people and their cheese and to stretch a simple parable to book length. At about a hundred pages, it is admittedly a short book (although it feels much, much longer, as it has so little meat and so much cheese).

It is a book that constantly strives for profundity and insight when its basic metaphor is not only silly but also misleading. Business isn't just about adapting to a changing world. In many cases, the existing business model is working fine and will continue to do so for decades; challenge is to find minor variations and to expand the existing customer base and markets, rather than getting on with 'finding some more cheese' somewhere else. Of course, there are also many examples of businesses that have had to adapt or people who created entirely new paradigms for business, but it is questionable whether such businesses would have much to learn from *Who Moved My Cheese?*.

The book starts with a group of classmates chatting about their lives after a high-school reunion. One of the group tells the others about an amazing story he has heard which has helped him to learn how to deal with change in his life and business. This introduces the actual parable, in which two mice (Sniff and Scurry) and two little people (Hem and Haw) live in a maze. They are used to finding their cheese in a particular location within the maze, but one day an invisible force moves the cheese. The mice, who are less analytical and judgemental than the little people, immediately set off looking for the cheese and quickly find it elsewhere in the maze. The little people find adapting to change to be a more complex challenge – they have more of their self-image and belief systems wrapped up in the cheese. (The cheese is used as a metaphor for anything of great importance, whether it be a job or relationship or the customer base of a sales team). Hem and Haw spend far too long debating whether or not to look elsewhere for cheese and wallowing in their anger at the unknown force that has moved their cheese.

Eventually, Haw decides to set out on a search for cheese elsewhere, while the more fearful Hem continues to stay put. At this stage Haw chisels the rather obvious message, 'If you do not change, you can become extinct', on the wall. When he does eventually find the cheese he takes some back for Hem, who refuses to share it. After reflecting on the situation, Haw chisels a few more platitudes on the wall, most of which are different ways of saying, 'Be prepared for change, don't be scared of it and constantly look for new sources of cheese.' Eventually even Hem realises he has been an idiot and Haw hears him approaching the most abundant source of cheese, 'Cheese Station N'.

Then the book returns to the classmates and they spend the rest of the book talking about the different things they have learned from the parable and suggest that it would be a good idea for any boss to distribute large quantities of the book to their employees as compulsory reading (a suggestion that regrettably was taken up by some businesses when the book was published, contributing to its mystifying success and sales of well over two million copies).

The final pages rather cheekily include an order form for further copies of the book as well as various bits of associated merchandise. The reader may not come away with their approach to change in the business environment transformed, as promised, but we do at least end up with a healthy regard for the sheer chutzpah of the author and publishers of this little book.

THE SPEED READ

Who Moved My Cheque?

Once there was a writer who was looking for a big cheque. He wrote a parable about some mice and some little people, but it wasn't quite cheesy enough and he didn't get a big cheque. Then he wrote about a group of people sitting around talking about how the parable had changed their lives and added an order form for his own book and, to everyone's astonishment, he did get a big cheque when his book infested bookshops and businesses around the world.

Common Sense on Mutual Funds

New Imperatives for the Intelligent Investor

John Bogle, 1999

John Bogle was the creator of the world's first index mutual fund in 1975 and, as the founder of the Vanguard Group, a hugely successful businessman and investor. This book lays out the basics of his approach to investment.

Bogle's key insight was that it is impossible for all managed funds to beat the market. Managed funds that sell the idea that they can do so are, to some extent, selling a dream. They can certainly beat the market for short spells, but they tend to be overhyped when they do so and to use such periods as the foundation of extensive marketing to bring in more investors to the fund and to justify high charges for those investors. Bogle argues that this in turn changes the relationship between the investor and the fund manager: 'Rather than being perceived as the owner of the fund, the shareholder is perceived as a mere customer of the adviser. At that point the mutual fund is no longer primarily an investment account under the stewardship of an investment manger, but an investment product under the control of a professional marketer.'

Either way, in the medium to long term there tends to be a reversion to the mean and in Bogle's view it is irrational to spend your time trying to pick the 'right' managed fund. It makes much more sense to invest in an index which tracks the entire market.

Bogle distinguished short-term speculation from genuine investment, which takes a longer-term view of the financial markets. His essential argument, as encapsulated in the title of the book, is that investors need to keep things simple and to act with common sense. To this end, he gives his basic rules of investing: concentrate on funds with low costs whenever you can; don't get taken in by investment advice that comes with hidden costs; don't focus too much on the past performance of a fund, other than as a basic yardstick as to their competence; ignore ratings systems that are based on stars; steer clear of large funds wherever possible; don't feel any need to spread your money across more than about five different funds; and, once you are invested, try to stick with the funds you have.

This latter point is particularly important when it comes to index fund investment. Since these funds will tend to match the market performance over the medium term, you are only degrading your prospects if you cash out of any funds that have a temporary dip (or if you attempt to take the profits from those which have had a good spell). The key to Bogle's approach to investment is to accept that no one can outguess the market and to be patient while avoiding incurring any unnecessary costs along the way.

As you read, you have to bear in mind that Bogle himself is selling something – the idea of the index funds that were the foundation of his own company and career. Having said that, his scathing critiques of the way that the financial industry generates profits for itself rather than for investors make for fascinating reading, as do his philosophical suggestions on how this might be reformed.

Not everyone is a fan of Bogle's investing strategy, but for straightforwardness and long-term performance, the evidence is that it is much more reliable than attempting to outperform the market through too much short-term chopping and changing.

THE SPEED READ

Common Sense on Mutual Funds

John Bogle, the inventor of the index mutual fund, lays out his basic thoughts on investing with simplicity. The basic message is that trying to outperform the market is a fool's errand but you can match the market and avoid unnecessary costs along the way by using a strategy based on index funds.

When Genius Failed

The Rise and Fall of Long-Term
Capital Management

Roger Lowenstein, 2000

In the aftermath of the global financial crisis that started in 2007, many asked why the financial and political elites seemed so unprepared for such an eventuality. If we want to look for warnings that were missed, one important example is the collapse of Long-Term Capital Management (LTCM) in 1998.

The hedge fund was founded in 1994 by John W. Meriwether, who had previously been head of bond trading at Salomon Brothers (and who featured in *Liar's Poker* by Michael Lewis). The directors of the board included the brilliant academics Myron S. Scholes and Robert C. Merton, who would jointly receive a Nobel Prize in economics in 1997 for devising new ways to 'determine the value of derivatives'. (Scholes had helped to devise the Black-Scholes model, while Merton had refined the mathematical foundations of the same model.)

The firm, which raised significant initial funds, was hugely profitable. It mainly relied on a combination of arbitrage, in which tiny differences in pricing of assets or of derivatives that track those assets, create the opportunity for risk-free profit, and leverage. Those tiny profits are made much larger by using borrowed money. Leverage, of course, magnifies downside risk as well as potential profits, but in the early years of the fund this risk was made to seem insignificant by the returns of 20–40 per cent per annum.

Problems gradually developed at the firm during 1997 and 1998, partly because of the Asian financial crisis and the Russian default and also as a result of other financial firms copying their business model, thus reducing the number of opportunities for genuine arbitrage. The company started taking bigger risks, still using massive leverage, and came unstuck as it lost over $4.5 billion in four months in 1998.

The Federal Reserve Bank, fearing a huge financial crisis if they allowed the firm to collapse in an unruly fashion, stepped in and twisted the arms of some of the major financial firms of Wall Street, many of whom already had money at stake, either directly or via the potential blowback effect on their own trading desks. LTCM was bailed out, using no public money, and was wound down, finally closing in 2000. There were concerns raised at the time that this was setting a bad precedent and creating a moral hazard for the future, but these fears were mostly dismissed because of the urgency of preventing an immediate market meltdown.

Some of the bets that had lost so much money ended up becoming profitable for the firms who bailed them out. But it was too late for LTCM, who had fallen victim partly because they had forgotten the wise words often attributed to John Maynard Keynes: 'Markets can remain irrational longer than you can remain solvent.' Some of those involved had their careers destroyed, but a surprising number of them lived to trade another day.

When Genius Failed is an unauthorised account of the firm, calling on interviews with many who worked there or were involved in the bailout. It is at its best when it is dealing with the people themselves and the way that the collapse went from unthinkable to inevitable in a few months of sudden shocks. *Inventing Money* by Nick Dunbar also tells the story of the LTCM crisis and is possibly a better book when it comes to explaining the nitty-gritty of the derivatives, how the Black-Scholes model worked in practice and so on. But that book is a more academic read and Lowenstein's book is the better one when it comes to the personalities involved and the wider context. His accounts of the panicky meetings of Wall Street executives with the Fed and the failure of last-minute rescue packages from Berkshire Hathaway, among others, give a good sense of the sheer drama of the story.

All the same, it is a long book, occasionally too loaded with detail. And there is a tendency to claiming wisdom after the event and to laying too much blame on mathematical modelling for the crisis (as opposed to the overconfidence LTCM showed in the models and the excessive additional risks they took when things started to go wrong). But it is well worth a read, as is Lowenstein's afterword in which he talks of LTCM as a template for future meltdowns, a canary in the coalmine that should not have been ignored.

It's arguable that the fact that the bailout didn't use public money and the way that some of the participants in the bailout ultimately avoided losses created a false sense of security. Either way, the hedge fund industry continued to operate with minimal regulation and the use of derivatives along with excessive leverage and the drive to deregulate the financial industry continued in the years after the collapse of LTCM.

So it is sombering to look back to the crisis now and see how many elements of the global financial crisis were prefigured in the course of this single business failure – and how few lessons were learned from it.

┌─ **THE SPEED READ** ───────────────────────┐

When Genius Failed

The story of the rise and fall of the hedge fund Long-Term Capital Management and in particular its collapse and subsequent bailout in 1998. A tragedy of hubris, greed and arrogance that should have been a warning of worse crises to come. Required reading for anyone who wants to understand how brilliant minds can invent seemingly foolproof solutions to problems that end up leading to disastrous outcomes, how mathematical modelling can lead to deeply illogical behaviour and how the best-laid schemes of mice and men often go awry.

└──┘

Business as Unusual

The Journey of Anita Roddick and the Body Shop

Anita Roddick, 2000

The iconic Body Shop had humble beginnings as a single small outlet in Brighton and went on to become a global brand. Roddick's book also charts the story of how her personal beliefs and politics came to embody the brand. It was a business approach that went against every norm in which modern corporate companies were usually created and operated and set out a new way of looking at the world through what eventually became known as ethical consumerism.

In this book, Roddick outlines her view that business should not be about money, it should instead be about responsibility. She places an emphasis on public good rather than private greed and it was her belief that business should be ethical that initially drove the Body Shop's success. In a way, the business was ahead of its time. Starting in 1976, its story reads more like today's fashionable start-ups whose goods are promoted as being ethically sourced. One modern equivalent is the rise of coffee-shop businesses in which the background story – where the coffee is grown and the people who grow it – is part of the marketing.

Roddick's business plans were always tied up with her own personal values and politics. She was anti-globalisation and concerned about the effect corporations were having on the environment. Her entrepreneurial success came from the way she branded the Body Shop from the start. She writes about how one shouldn't be a 'nondescript' person or one will get a 'nondescript' product. She also encourages everyone to question what they are told, investigate it and if necessary challenge it. It is this emphasis on being fearless when setting up a business that drove her to success.

The first Body Shop was set up as an unconventional beauty and cosmetics shop. Roddick had very little money: the now iconic green paint was originally chosen to cover up the damp on the walls. She didn't have enough money for bottles and so started offering customers refills in their own bottles at a discount. While this was opportunistic, it established recycling as part of the business model and this worked to promote her environmental political views.

She contacted a local herbalist to create her products, having had the idea for them while travelling through developing countries, observing the ingredients local women used in their products. Her travels also gave her the inspiration for her business as one that gave back to the world community rather than one that simply generated profit.

One of the keys to her success was the way the Body Shop was branded and marketed. Roddick's profits-with-a-principle attitude helped her gain publicity and made people feel good about buying her products. Eschewing conventional marketing, she became her own PR for the company through political campaigning. She rallied publicly for the causes she believed in. The Body Shop opposed testing on animals and sold itself on this basis. Through its Trade Not Aid mission it helped developing economies by buying its products and packaging from them and making their backstories known through packaging and informational leaflets and posters. Roddick supported Save the Whale rallies and the Body Shop's products for children came with informative storybooks about endangered animals throughout the world.

At the same time, hers was a business model focused as much on selling as it was on raising social awareness of issues around the world. Roddick's very public political campaigning not only drew attention to various causes, it also raised awareness of the brand too. Political awareness became the brand and its success was built around the fact that by buying the products, people felt they were in some way helping the causes that the company campaigned for. The Body Shop not only used recyclable materials and natural products, its social messages were also displayed on the T-shirts worn by staff. At the time there were a lot of shopping boycotts in England: for instance, consumers refused to buy products from South Africa because of their support for the anti-apartheid movement. Political awareness was fashionable and the Body Shop's success capitalised on this.

The idea of knowing the source of the product you are buying, where it was made and by whom is now a growing part of consumer culture. People are much more aware of ethical causes and many businesses are now using this as a selling point. By turning her political beliefs into a growing business Anita Roddick was one of the pioneers who showed that acting ethically and making a profit were not mutually exclusive.

Business as Unusual

The story of Anita Roddick and the early years of her Body Shop business. She also lays out her basic business values:

- Aim for profits with a principle.
- Use your political beliefs to raise awareness of the brand.
- Promote yourself through social campaigning rather than through conventional advertising.
- Tell the backstory to the products you are marketing.
- Source your products ethically, support the communities that produce them.
- Make your message clear in packaging and branding within your business.
- Don't be nondescript, be someone with a visible presence, someone who will be listened to.
- Challenge things you disagree with.
- You are never too small to make a success of it.

How to Become a Rainmaker

The Rules for Getting and
Keeping Customers and Clients

Jeffrey J. Fox, 2000

In business, a 'rainmaker' is an individual who brings in new business and new accounts so successfully that it almost looks like magic. *How to Become a Rainmaker* purports to be a guide to how to become such an individual, though it is probably better approached as a quirky but occasionally useful manual on the art of salesmanship in general.

Jeffrey J. Fox is also the author of *How to Become CEO* (good luck with that one . . .), *Dollarization Discipline* and numerous other snappily titled business books. He writes in short, thought-provoking chapters that often come with intentionally counter-intuitive titles such as 'Dare to be dumb' and 'Love voicemail'. He is fond of Dale Carnegie-style parables of, for instance, the teenager who took the wonderful advice of one of her customers on how to make an impression and is now the most popular babysitter in town.

If the style of the book doesn't want to make you scream, and it may well do, there is actually some good advice in here, at least if you think about the overall approach Fox is talking about. He often focuses on details, such as where to sit in a restaurant, parking at the back of the parking area so your customer doesn't see your awkward exit from your vehicle, remembering that the customer is more interested in themselves than you and knowing that asking a lot of questions can sometimes elicit that useful nugget of information that your competitors missed. (The latter is the point of the chapter 'Dare to be dumb' in which he spins the tale of a salesperson who asks lots of questions and thereby finds a selling opportunity.) And he also encourages the salesperson to be as prepared as possible, giving advice such as, 'Always taste the wine before a wine-tasting' (to avoid one bad bottle ruining the entire event).

He includes minor bits of advice such as never putting a pen in your pocket, because it could leak and ruin your shirt, making you look incompetent in your meeting. You'd hope that most people worked this out at school, but if they didn't it is sensible to think about these kinds of details about how you will come across in a sales scenario and to be prepared for all options.

It's easy to mock this book, but the basic message here is actually very sound. Good salespeople think through all of these kinds of details and options in advance and rehearse in their heads the sorts of questions they might ask and how they might steer the conversation in productive directions. It's probably best to ignore some of the details of what Fox suggests. For instance, he tells you that you are not at a lunch meeting to have lunch itself and should not waste a single minute eating when you could be selling. Which in many cases would come across as pretty creepy and weird – most people expect lunch to be at least partially a social occasion, with business only being a part of the equation and relationship-building being the larger part.

Similarly, he advises sitting with your back to the wall in the restaurant so that your customer is completely focused on you, as you relentlessly sell, sell, sell to them. And when it comes to loving voicemail, what starts out as a counter-intuitive claim just ends up sounding like plain bad advice as he tells you to use little prepared speeches and gives an example which would be as infuriating as the clumsiest of spam phone calls to most listeners. (Admittedly, the book is from the turn of the millennium, before spam calls proliferated, so he can perhaps be excused on this point.)

In the end, this is a short book that can be read in a couple of hours, so the best approach is probably to read it and listen to some of the best advice while being sceptical of the parts that don't ring true. Several of the chapters are simply 'killer sales questions', such as suggesting a potential customer 'give your product a try' (on the basis that this doesn't feel like a big commitment but could lead to one anyway). They are actually pretty smart and well-explained. And if the book does nothing else, it will make anyone in a sales job think hard about what they are getting right and wrong in their own approach to calls and meetings.

You might not actually become a rainmaker after reading this book. But, if you don't take Fox's claims too seriously, you might still become a more organised, prepared sales-person and that is no bad thing.

How to Become a Rainmaker

If you want to be a rainmaker, to bring in wondrous amounts of new business and new contacts to your company, then you need to focus on every detail of your approach, from how you dress and what you eat through to understanding every detail of the business of potential clients.

If you listen to all of the advice in this book and go to lunch without eating lunch and leave a lot of cheesy sales voicemails, you are unlikely to become a rainmaker. But if you take on board the overall theme of preparation and focus and adapt it to your own particular circumstances, and if you are selective about the tips in the book, then it can be useful. A reminder to review your own sales performance and to avoid basic errors like turning up to a sales meeting with ink or coffee all over your clothing.

Play Like a Man, Win Like a Woman

What Men Know About Success
That Women Need to Learn

Gail Evans, 2000

Gail Evans was the first female executive vice president at CNN and wrote this book as a guide for other potential women leaders on how to reach the top relatively unscathed within a male-dominated, competitive environment.

Evans sees the world of business as a game, one which men know the rules for (since they made them) and that women need to learn how to play if they want success. She argues that she isn't advocating that all women need to play exactly by men's rules since women have many inherent traits that they can use to their advantage in the workplace. She does, however, maintain that there are basic rules that women need to acquaint themselves with. This has earned her much criticism from women reviewers for aiming to fit in with the status quo rather than striving to change it, but this is nevertheless a well-known book on women in business and one example of the difficulty women writers have found in squaring the circle of how to both fit in with and challenge misogynist assumptions in the workplace.

Her key points are that you should send out the right message about yourself and that you are who you say you are, so pick your goal and convince yourself you can achieve it. Never succumb to the role of victim and be direct about what you want. For Evans, men's sense of fulfilment comes from what they make, while women's sense of achievement comes from what they do. For her, this is one example of women not doing things the way men do. She states that men can reconcile themselves to doing work that doesn't make them happy by getting high-profile rewards while women tend to find something they like doing and stay there. This is perhaps a bit of stereotyping but Evans insists there are consequences for not playing by the 'rules'. So women must take charge of their own destiny.

Evans's biggest recommendation for women is not to make things too personal. She suggests that women's inclination to form friendly relationships at work hampers their success because it can lead them to interpret basic information in personal terms. Her famous quote, 'Work isn't a sorority', is in reference to this tendency. Once again the critics are quick to point out her 'allowances' for male behaviour. Men are allowed to be rude, ugly, arrogant and wrong in their judgements. Women are not. Men are allowed to form sexual relationships at work whereas for women this tends to end badly. But Evans's point seems to be that these things all too quickly become personal for women. A mistake takes on the mantle of personal failure; a friendship becomes a personal crutch that prevents someone from applying for that promotion or advancement; not looking your best can display a lack of a sense of self-worth and an office fling becomes a potential love affair. In each of these scenarios, women invest far more personally and emotionally than do men and for Evans these are dangers that hold them back on the career ladder.

She also advises women to be flexible when setting their goals. Inflexibility impedes their ability to consider new possibilities. For Evans, a good player has the ability to improvise and has the vision to see the long game and how to get the results they want. But she once again refers to women's need for friendship in this section by pointing out that work is not about friendship, just as team sport isn't. You have to know and understand your teammates but they don't have to be your friends. Evans claims that men disagree about job-related matters and see it as simply arguing sporting tactics whereas women are quick to point the finger at a colleague who disagrees with them as being disloyal or unsupportive.

Evans also advises women to accept uncertainty and not be afraid of the practice of making it up as you go along. She suggests that men enter the workplace already confident and so they have a much better chance of success. Conversely, women often enter the workplace with a sense of being an impostor, having to act the part and being unsure of themselves and their role. Women tend towards a desire for perfection, whereas men don't. She emphasises that everyone is an impostor but while men know it and have become adept at faking it, women don't and so fail to make the same gains. Her advice is to rely on improvisation and self-confidence.

Women also need to think more about how to compartmentalise rather than multitask. In Evans's view, men don't get distracted by the bigger picture but women do and this can lead to unnecessary stress. She advocates using humour to diffuse difficult situations but once again points out that women tend to use humour differently and must learn to use it as men do. For Evans, women's humour tends to be observational, but for men it is situational and it is this ability to raise humour from a situation that makes men better at getting ahead through difficult situations in the workplace.

At times, the whole purpose of this book seems to be to point out that business is a world made by men and that women must understand how men operate in order to succeed. It was this that set Evans up for a lot of criticism but some of the advice on not taking things too personally is actually useful. If a bit outdated, her view – that women in the workplace are often seen by men as mother, daughter, sister, wife or mistress and that women must avoid becoming victim to these roles – is a reminder that some men may be unconsciously referring to these stereotypes in workplace interactions rather than seeing an equal business colleague as they would in a man. This can at least help women to avoid falling into any unforeseen traps where they react according to the role allocated and to fulfil Evans's advice that they should take charge of their own destiny.

THE SPEED READ

Play Like a Man, Win Like a Woman

A guide for women on how to succeed in a workplace that can often be dominated by men and macho values. Send out the right message about yourself and your goals – you are who you say you are. Don't fall into a 'role' allocated to you, don't be a victim, take charge of your own destiny. Don't take things personally – it's about business, not you.

Work is not the place to find friends but to secure teammates. Do not invest too much emotionally. Be flexible in your goals: always be open to new possibilities. Everyone is an impostor, so accept uncertainty and display self-confidence. Don't be a perfectionist – compartmentalise and focus on the job to hand. Maintain a sense of humour about things, especially when it is specific to a particular situation.

The Tipping Point

How Little Things Can Make a Big Difference

Malcolm Gladwell, 2000

This is one of those books that contain one big idea that business people should be aware of. Opinion is divided as to whether it is good in other respects.

Many people enjoy Gladwell's chatty, anecdotal approach, which takes in everything from the market research carried out by the creators of *Sesame Street* to the 'broken windows' theory of social disorder, to the sudden rise in popularity of Hush Puppies in the 1990s. As a result, his books have sold huge quantities. But he has his critics, including those scientists who feel his interpretations of data can lack rigour and that he therefore draws some conclusions that are not justified by the evidence. And there are cynics who grumble that Gladwell's big idea was more about how to take scientific ideas and transmute them into a best-seller (thus reaching his own 'tipping point') than it was about communicating accurate scientific knowledge.[1]

---

[1] See for instance: Steven Pinker, 'Malcolm Gladwell, Eclectic Detective' in *The New York Times*, 7 November 2009; and Christopher Chabris, 'The Trouble With Malcolm Gladwell' in *Slate Magazine*, 8 October 2013

Either way, the big idea that readers should be aware of is one that relates to Richard Dawkins' earlier writing on 'memes', cultural ideas and the ways that they are transmitted through society.[2] Gladwell focuses on the ways that an idea can start with a small number of people and how it becomes 'sticky' to the point that it becomes an 'epidemic'.

For Gladwell, there are three different kinds of people who are important in the creation of this kind of tipping point. 'Connectors' are the people who have many connections through which they can pass on their enthusiasms and ideas. 'Mavens' are those who have the knowledge and authority to let people know whether something works or not and what the best price or product is, and to pass on other types of information within the marketplace. 'Salesmen' can persuade people to believe in a new product or idea.

He explores the ways in which these three groups interact and how it can lead to the sudden explosion of interest when a tipping point is reached. He goes on to a discussion of the S-curve which ideas tend to follow – starting with innovators, then early adopters, then an 'early majority' and, finally, the 'late majority' (the point at which many ideas or products can start to lose their appeal to the more fashionable early adopters).

A problem with the book from a business point of view is that it doesn't provide a huge amount of information on how to go about creating a tipping point. Of course, we all know that for something to 'go viral', a lot of conditions need to be met and some of them are beyond anyone's control. But Gladwell's book is more concerned with *ex post facto* explanations of tipping points than analysing how to make them happen.

---

[2] Richard Dawkins, *The Selfish Gene* (1976), OUP, Oxford, 2016, p.104

He does have some other useful anecdotes that can be relevant to business: for instance, the detail about companies such as Gore and Associates (famous for the material Gore-Tex) breaking a company into smaller units when employing more than 150 people (because it is hard for anyone to truly know or connect with more than that many people). But on the whole it is hard to take a moral from this book on how to market products in a way that maximises their chances of creating an 'epidemic' effect.

The other problem with *The Tipping Point* is that, while 2000 isn't such a long time ago, the world of social media in particular has been completely transformed. Some of the material can seem downright quaint, especially with regards to how quickly a tipping point can occur. We are increasingly used to memes going viral in the course of a few hours and being 'so last year' a few days later.

However, that doesn't necessarily mean that this book has become obsolete – the process by which things become viral today is essentially the same, it is just that the rapid flow of information means that it has become accelerated to a scarcely believable degree and it is even more necessary for companies to have an understanding of how tipping points come about. So Gladwell's thesis is still relevant, but if you want advice on creating a tipping point, there are other books on marketing and social media that will be of more practical use.

The Tipping Point

Products and ideas can reach a 'tipping point' and reach 'epidemic' proportions (or 'go viral' in contemporary description) when the right conditions are met. The three key types of individuals who contribute to a tipping point are 'connectors' (who communicate with many people), 'mavens' (who disseminate information) and 'salesmen' (who persuade people to believe in an idea). Malcolm Gladwell's book reached its own tipping point when it became a best-seller, but it can be argued that it is outdated now that the world of information and social media moves so much faster than it did when this book was written.

Good to Great

Why Some Companies Make the Leap . . . and Others Don't

Jim Collins, 2001

In 1994, Jim Collins' book *Built to Last* was published. Based on a six-year research project into how companies actually work, it was about the qualities that make great companies endure. But as this book didn't really answer the question of how companies become great in the first place, he returned with *Good to Great* in 2001.

The basic idea for the book is a clever one, which accounts for its huge success: Collins and his team analysed the forty-year performance of over 1,400 companies and came up with a shortlist of eleven that had gone from being merely good to great. They then attempted to identify what they had in common.

Collins' explanation of their similarities relies on numerous analogies and buzzwords (to an occasionally tiresome degree). Firstly, he dismisses many of the ways in which companies attempt to become great – through acquisitions, superstar CEOs, huge salary bonus structures, massive programmes of change or as a response to a major crisis that motivates the workforce. Instead, he compares the process of change to waiting for an egg to hatch or to attempting to get a huge, horizontally mounted flywheel to turn. The latter task might take the concerted efforts of many individuals over an extended period before the spinning of the wheel becomes really impressive. He contrasts this Flywheel Effect with the Doom Loop, in which companies attempt to enact change through sudden lurches of direction or diktats from management.

In order to achieve such patient, diligent change, Collins argues that you need to 'get the right people on the bus' before you identify the direction of travel. In other words, you need to hire good people who will work hard and co-operate (which may be incredibly obvious, but is still sound advice).

Moving on from flywheels and buses, Collins contrasts foxes and hedgehogs, using the old analogy of foxes having a lot of different ideas while hedgehogs have one big concept. For a company to go from good to great, he argues, it needs a leader (preferably a 'level five leader', a concept he is very fond of but that seems hard to pin down in practice) who can identify the company's Hedgehog Concept. This requires them to ask the brutal questions like, 'What are we good at doing?' and, 'What will we never be the best at doing?' and to focus the company solely on the things that the company can become great at doing. (I didn't mention that identifying the Hedgehog Concept requires a diagram of three intersecting circles: I'm skipping a bit to try to avoid total jargon overload . . .)

The company needs a List of Things to Stop Doing. Collins gives the example of Kimberly-Clark, whose CEO realised they were capable of being best in the world in the consumer paper business, having built the Kleenex brand, and as a result chose to exit the paper mills industry, where most of the company's revenues had previously been generated. Eventually, they did become hugely successful in this area, although it was a long and slow process.

This is a case of Collins' thinking being illuminating. Many of us will have worked in companies where huge effort and resources went into a part of the business that had only limited growth potential or was in slow decline and will have seen how hard it is for a CEO to make the decision to stop doing that thing. (It is also an example which makes you ponder how scientific the research really is – because a company which made a similar, but less fortunate choice to stop doing something could easily be castigated for being in the Doom Loop, something that Collins slams.)

Apart from the irritating jargon, the main reason to be sceptical about this book is how poorly, in the years following the book's publication, some of the companies described as great have performed. Gillette, Walgreens, Wells Fargo and a few others continued to do well enough, though on the whole the group of eleven companies profiled here underperformed the S&P average. And it is jarring to see Fannie Mae, which was to crash and burn within the decade, lionised as a great success, while Circuit City got into serious trouble within a few years. It is revealing that Collins' 2009 book *How the Mighty Fall* had to deal with the fact that eleven out of sixty companies identified in his earlier books as 'great' were now no better than mediocre.

Part of the explanation is that lack of true scientific rigour. Collins and his team may have identified some companies that did well in the same period, but it is a strong claim to make to say that he can identify the exact reasons and, since they haven't looked for counter-examples or false positives, it is impossible to say how many other companies did exactly the same things and failed to go from 'good to great'.

In addition, many of the claims made by Collins on behalf of these companies are pretty nebulous. Hiring the right people is something that any company will strive to do, for obvious reasons. Being patient and diligent are clearly good values, although in a world where CEOs and management teams regularly rotate, it can be hard to achieve in practice. And confronting brutal facts is clearly going to be part of the career profile of any aspiring CEO, but it doesn't really help us to know which CEOs will make the *right* decisions having done so.

The danger here is that the pseudo-scientific rigour of the book's approach can blind readers to the lack of genuine scientific analysis. It is best to read this only while bearing in mind that, with hindsight, any of us can say which companies succeeded and which failed – and that explaining why is not necessarily as easy as it looks.

THE SPEED READ

Good to Great

An attempt to analyse the reasons why some companies make the leap forwards from being good companies to great ones. Having compared the fortunes of hundreds of companies, Collins narrows the list down to eleven companies who had seen notable success over recent decades. His prescription for making the good-to-great transition is based on advice like staying focused on what the company does best, hiring good people, being patient and diligent, but never complacent and to have 'level five leaders' who aren't ego-driven in their decision-making. There's also a lot of jargon and folksy analogies along the way. There are two big problems: firstly, that this advice is all pretty nebulous and bland; it would be hard to find any good companies that didn't believe they were acting this way already. And, secondly, that so many of the companies Collins identified as great rapidly turned out to be not so great or, in the case of Fannie Mae, actually quite disastrous. So what started out seeming like an ice-cold piece of scientific analysis ends up feeling more like just a load of hot air.

Getting Things Done

The Art of Stress-free Productivity

David Allen, 2001

This is not so much a business book as a book about personal organisation. The hypothesis is that if you organise the small things you have to do then you will free your mind of clutter and become more productive in general. The updated 2015 version includes more options for the digital age: software and smartphones have made it much easier to be organised and Allen has included tips on how to get the best out of these new devices, although there is still advice about keeping files and organising paperwork from the original.

Allen suggests a five-stage approach to managing your things-to-do. The first involves 'collecting' items that need your attention (later editions use different terms for essentially the same processes). Once you have done this you are ready to start the 'processing' stage. Processing involves going through those things one by one and deciding what your next action with them will involve. Following on from this is 'taking action'. You also need to 'organise' your results and then 'review' your options for dealing with them. He stresses the need to prioritise, by acting immediately if you can or filing something, discarding it or creating what the author calls a 'next action' – putting it aside to follow up later, if this is possible.

The author suggests spending two days doing the initial organising and then constantly reviewing your organising to get the optimum benefit from your new-found proficiency. There is a lot of stress placed on writing lists, checking those lists frequently and creating a filing system to deal with your lists. This approach may free up your mind but it does seem to demand a lot of your time in the process.

He stresses the importance of judging priorities according to context: for instance, if you need to make a phone call or send an email and are near a device that enables you to do that, then do it immediately and cross it off your list. The idea being that the more things you deal with immediately without procrastination, the more effectively you will free up that 'cluttered' mind.

It has to be admitted that many people have found this book and the Getting Things Done system extremely helpful. But it won't be to everyone's taste. There is a danger that the book encourages people to become automatons and the emphasis on being in control is sometimes taken to a comical extreme. If we imagine someone who follows Allen's advice to the letter, this would be a person surrounded by lists, box files with titles such as 'What the cat likes on Tuesdays' and 'Thursday is green salad day', endless Post-it notes and filing trays full of every kind of minutiae that everyday mundane situations can throw up. If you want to operate like a computer system, appear very controlling and, yes, let's say it, are ever so slightly neurotic, then maybe this is the perfect book for you.

Getting Things Done

In order to unclutter your mind you need to develop external systems for keeping everything organised so that you can focus on the task at hand without distractions. Collect together all items that need your attention. Process these things one by one and decide what needs immediate action and what can be put in your in-tray to follow up next. Review your system constantly, refine it and improve it. Create files (these can be digital or manual depending on your preference). If you can do something immediately, do it and cross it off your list. Spend two minutes every day writing a to-do list and dealing with it. Declutter your mind of all those little things you have to do and you will be better able to see the big picture and reach your goal . . . And don't forget to switch yourself off at the end of the day.

Boo Hoo

A Dot Com Story from Concept to Catastrophe

Ernst Malmsten, 2001

This is the cautionary tale of the rise and fall of the fashion retail website business boo.com, which was founded in 1999 by Malmsten, Kajsa Leander and Patrik Hedelin.

Malmsten and Leander had previously run the successful online book retailer bokus.com, which they sold in 1998, making them millionaires. It was partly because their previous venture into online retail had been so successful that they were seen as embodying the new age of companies, and it was that coupled with their vision of boo.com as a global brand that persuaded investors to give them $135 million.

Their vision was indeed ambitious. Beginning in Carnaby Street in London with forty employees, they soon had over four hundred staff in several countries and that was before the website was even close to launching. While the book is occasionally hilarious, Malmsten comes across as remarkably arrogant in both his vision of himself as a successful businessman and in the amount of blame he is prepared to lay at the feet of others for the ultimate failure of his business.

The funding was largely spent as soon as it is was acquired: huge payouts were given to IT consultants and the business owners seemed to take Concorde to New York every other week. A huge amount of money was spent staying in five-star hotels and on stylists and hairdressers. It almost seems as though they believed that if they acted the part, the rest would follow.

As a result, there seems to have been more time spent on creating the vision of the brand than on the actual logistics of running a business. They created a virtual online assistant called Miss Boo and wanted a 3D imaging process on the website where Miss Boo would get an item of clothing for you, then place it on a mannequin so you could view it from all angles. This was exciting technology for the late 1990s and it was partly this that got investors so enthusiastic. They didn't, however, make sufficient allowances for 1990s internet speeds: the website was slow to load and didn't work at all on some slower modems (a notice added to the homepage pointed out that it only worked on modems with a 56K download speed, which was unusually fast for the time). Despite increasing amounts of money thrown at IT specialists, the launch was postponed on a number of occasions. Meanwhile, an 'international hairstylist' was brought in to design hairstyles for Miss Boo.

At the same time, the company launched the online fashion magazine Boom, recruiting known writers from *Vanity Fair* and *Vogue*. The magazine was launched in several European countries so had to be written in different languages, adding to payroll costs that were already spiralling out of control. And still this was all before the site (the actual business) was even launched. Once that did finally happen, the technical problems became self-evident.

The complex online shopping experience visualised by Malmsten and his partners meant that the site was hard to navigate and many people couldn't access it because of the loading problems. Boo.com also offered free returns, although their logistics company were charging the business significant amounts. They had grown too large too quickly and didn't take into account the finer details of selling clothing online – such as problems with suppliers and returns which were always likely to run at a higher rate for fashion items than they had for other successful online selling ventures like Amazon with its books.

When cashflow became an obvious concern, Malmsten blamed Leander for insisting that the online international fashion magazine was essential to the business and couldn't be scaled back. A former model herself, this seems to have been her pet project within the company. They also hadn't sufficiently taken into account fluctuating prices of brands in different countries and this led to further supply problems. Unsurprisingly, funders began to get worried and started to pull their money out. Malmsten refuses to take any blame in his writing and merely suggests that the banks had an agenda and were against him.

He wrote the book to 'capture all the broken dreams of the dot com era'. It certainly does that. It is a reminder of a time when anything seemed possible and any dream could come true. The founders certainly had big dreams but they didn't look carefully enough at the finer details (especially the technical ones); they also completely failed to control costs or to spend money in proportion to the actual size of the business prior to its launch. The moral of the story is: if you want to launch a business of any size you need to keep control of costs, understand every detail and, above all, not have an ego the size of a planet.

┌─ **THE SPEED READ** ─────────────────────────────

Boo Hoo

The story of a huge online business failure and a reminder of
the madness of the dot-com bubble in the late 1990s, from
which any wannabe entrepreneur can learn a few lessons.

If you set up an online company, focus and start small,
even if you dream big. Don't overspend before you see some
returns on your business. Don't spend your investment
money on frequent long-haul flights and five-star hotels,
at least until your business is successful ... And, if your
business fails, remember, there is always somebody to
blame (and it's probably not you).

Crucial Conversations

Tools for Talking When Stakes Are High

Kerry Patterson, Joseph Grenny, Ron McMillan,
Al Switzler, 2002

One problem that most people face in the workplace is how to deal with difficult conversations. These can range from asking your boss for a pay rise and dealing with inappropriate behaviour in colleagues to asking an employee to improve their performance. And there are many other situations in which we know we need to have a conversation which, deep down, we are dreading.

This is a book aimed at helping people to deal with those conversations and to understand what is happening in them. The authors start out by defining what a crucial conversation is: one in which the stakes are relatively high, the participants have differing opinions and strong emotions are attached. They also acknowledge that humans haven't evolved to be great at dealing with such conversations – our reaction to emotional discomfort is a physical one, in which our heart rate increases and our adrenaline levels rise and this tends to trigger our fight-or-flight response. Or, in the jargon preferred by the authors, we tend to lapse into 'violence or silence'.

This leads us to one of the weaker points of the book, its tendency to boil everything down into catchphrases or acronyms. They tell us to 'start with heart', ask us to consider our 'style under stress' and so on. The authors all work for the same corporate consultancy (which develops training programmes) and one often feels that the lessons in the book have been derived from PowerPoint presentations with their handy mnemonics. However, if that doesn't put you off, there is some genuinely useful content here.

From the start, the authors stress the importance of not giving in to the urge to avoid difficult conversations, pointing out how much can go wrong if problems are not confronted. (The book also deals with issues in personal relationships and with ethical situations, such as nurses who may be fearful about talking to a doctor about that doctor's unsafe practices.) They discuss a situation in which a spouse is upset by their partner's distant behaviour – however, rather than expressing this clearly and calmly, they resort to sarcasm and nasty digs which then compound the problem, thus creating a vicious circle. They stress that people often feel that they have to choose between keeping a friend and telling the truth and argue that the purpose of the book is to show you how to escape from that feeling and have the courage to deal with issues that need addressing.

The point about 'starting with heart' is that you need to start from a position of self-awareness about what you feel about an issue and to separate feelings of anger or self-interest from your broader understanding of the issue. So you need to work on the 'me' part of the equation first – what you want for yourself, for the other person and for the relationship in general.

'Learn to look' – in other words, observe how the other person is reacting. For this you need a strong understanding of all the signs that people are retreating into silence (or other ways of refusing to communicate) or violence, which can also include modes of communication such as sarcasm or passive-aggressive behaviour.

Next you need to find ways to 'make the conversation safe' – to find ways of seeking permission to have the conversation, to have it at an appropriate time and in the right setting and to make it clear that you are looking for mutual solutions. For this you also need to be on top of all the facts and the possible narratives and to have a clear understanding of the possible arguments and defences that face you. You also need to give the other party or parties room to make their points and not to feel you have to railroad them into accepting your version of the story.

The final stage of the process is about how you conclude a conversation and commit to actions to remedy the problems that have been discussed. As the authors point out, finishing a difficult conversation without some kind of commitment to a mutual path forwards can leave things worse than they were before.

It is sometimes possible to state the message of a book in a few hundred words without losing anything important. However, in the case of this book, the detail is the really important part. It is in providing specific examples and analysis of the ways in which crucial conversations can go well or badly that the book really shines. It is a book that can be highly recommended for anyone who has ever avoided a difficult conversation or can see that they made mistakes in the way they dealt with an interpersonal problem at work. Careful study of the book won't turn you into the greatest negotiator in the world overnight, but it will certainly help you to realise what you have been doing wrong and to get more of those difficult conversations right in future.

THE SPEED READ

Crucial Conversations

An extremely useful manual for dealing with difficult conversations in the workplace and elsewhere. The natural human response to such situations is to fight or run away, and when we try to talk in spite of those urges we can make mistakes. The authors advise that you should start by understanding your own motivations and desires in the situation, then learn to clearly observe the other person's reactions. Then you need to make the context for the conversation a 'safe' one, to state your case clearly, listen well to their points and agree to mutual action in conclusion. However, in this case a short summary of the book is insufficient, and for maximum effect it would be advisable to read the full version.

Anyone Can Do It

Building Coffee Republic from Our Kitchen Table –
57 Real-Life Laws on Entrepreneurship

Sahar and Bobby Hashemi, 2002

Siblings Sahar and Bobby Hashemi built up UK high-street chain Coffee Republic from scratch after they both gave up highly paid jobs to pursue their dream. In this book they tell their story and give some advice for others wanting to do the same thing.

It's worth knowing that they were far from penniless when they started out: they were given £10,000 by their parents (not a loan but a gift) and most of their friends seem to be high-flying business lawyers or investment bankers. They did give up working for a year, but they still managed to live in a house in upmarket Kensington and to pay all their bills. So it's not really the rags-to-riches tale it promises, apart from the fact that neither of them knew anything about running a coffee shop when they started.

This is a mixture of memoir, telling the story of how they set up the business, and self-help guide, motivating people to have a go and start up their own business (providing you have the friends and the contacts, obviously). The book is structured around their laws of entrepreneurship and they also list eight habits that they believe can lead anyone to success.

The first of these habits is belief. This is where the idea that 'anyone can do it' comes into play. They argue that we are all creative, but only some of us practice and learn how to be creative. This is the key to developing your vision. Secondly, see the world from your customers' point of view: what do they need and hope for from the product you are creating? Don't rely on market research – experience the world in which you want your product to succeed first-hand.

Thirdly, go out and see what the competition is like; don't sit at home writing business plans at your desk. They frequently advise the reader to get out and experience things rather than sit and imagine them and warn against relying on the skills and experience you already have because that may prevent you from forming new ideas. (Since neither of them had run a coffee shop before this may seem pretty obvious advice: they would have had to see how coffee shops operated before committing to anything, as would anyone branching out in a completely new direction.)

They recommend an agile approach to business because start-ups often fail and if they do you have to regroup and move on with a new idea. This trial and error style of doing business is becoming more and more indispensable, particularly among start-ups, in an ever-changing economic climate. And like many other business gurus over the years, they recommend not taking 'No' for an answer and persevering until you get to be where you want to be. They also recommend 'boot-strapping', which is basically making the most of the resources you have and getting them to stretch as far as possible. Lastly, enjoy your work so that you take 100 per cent of yourself into the business each day. Anyone who doesn't enjoy their work, according to the Hashemis, is holding themselves back. Automatons do not work well for a start-up business, so to create one you need to think less like a corporate drone and more creatively.

Throughout the book, the authors stress the need to ask, 'Why?', both when things go well and when they don't, as this is the way to learn and improve. They also see adaptability as a virtue, as setting up a business is a long process of trial and error. If something doesn't work, you need to be agile and turn to something else. Don't be afraid to abandon your original plan if it doesn't seem to be working. If it does work, continuously develop it. Become your own customer base and think how you would like things to progress.

If you take out the personal experience stories and make allowances for the fact that not everyone has as privileged a start from which to build a business, this is a useful basic guide to the things you will need to think about when setting up a business. All businesses face different challenges, but there is always value in reading about how particular entrepreneurs faced their challenges and went on to create a successful business.

However, an extra caveat is that Coffee Republic ended up having a pretty chequered history: they almost went under in 2001 when they overexpanded, Sahar left the company not long after that, Bobby was thrown out by shareholders in 2006 and the chain went into administration in 2009. From 187 outlets in the UK the business, under the new owners, currently has fifty-two. As is often the case, the kind of energy and skills that allow for the creation of a start-up business seem not to have translated into a stable long-term business plan.

Anyone Can Do It

We set up a successful business from scratch – in fact, anyone can do it and so can you (if you have the finances and connections). Be your own customer in order to see what needs developing. Go out and do some research in the field. Accept that you don't know everything and learn. Keep asking, 'Why?', when things go wrong or well. Be adaptable and prepare to change things if they aren't working. Never take 'No' for an answer. Make the most of the resources you have. Make sure you enjoy what you are doing and give 100 per cent of yourself to your job.

The Corporation

The Pathological Pursuit of Profit and Power

Joel Bakan, 2003

The Corporation is an alternative take on the world of business which argues that corporations have become inherently dangerous institutions because of the legal status they have acquired over the last century or so. It is an interesting and challenging read for anyone who has wondered whether the world of business needs absolute and fundamental reform in order to be fit for purpose.

One of the refreshing things about Bakan's book is that he explicitly avoids criticising the people who work for corporations. He also based his work on interviews from across the political spectrum, including Milton Friedman, Noam Chomsky and the experienced business consultant and author Peter Drucker (see p. 47).

Corporations have been granted the status of being a 'person' under the law, for reasons that are entirely understandable – the whole concept of limited liability requires shareholders to be protected when taking reasonable risks. However, corporations are also governed by laws that require them to base their entire business practice on the pursuit of profit. Apart from following government-imposed regulations, of course, their one imperative is to pursue profit regardless of the social and environmental costs. This is the duty they legally owe to their shareholders. Modern corporations may make a fuss about the sustainable or worthy initiatives they are launching in poor communities or in the developing world, but they are simultaneously required to present these endeavours to the shareholders as being for purely profitable purposes, thus undermining any claims or desire to do genuine good through philanthropic or charitable activities.

Similarly disturbing are examples of automobile companies undertaking cost/benefit analysis to decide whether the cost of remedying a faulty fuel-tank design that might kill drivers and passengers outweighs the costs of paying out on lawsuits to the families of those who might end up being killed. Again, ethics takes a second place to efficiency and profit in such callous equations.

As a result, Bakan regards the modern corporation as being akin to a psychopath, since they are forced to behave in a psychopathic manner, pursuing private gain at any cost to other entities in the world. And he regards public protest and pressure as insufficient to change this, since the psychopathic nature of the corporation is innate due to their legal status.

For a small- or medium-business owner, this is an interesting read because of the contrast between the behaviour that is required of corporate boards and managers and the relative freedom smaller businesses have to pursue a more sustainable path – it would certainly make anyone who was considering taking a private company into public ownership wonder whether they were doing the right thing. For anyone who feels that their small or local business is at threat because of competition from corporations, the idea that the corporation is innately flawed is likely to be an appealing one. For a consumer faced with choices between local and multinational businesses, this may add more incentive to side with the smaller business. And even for the purist free-market capitalist, the explanation of the way in which international systems have been warped to favour one specific type of business should give pause for thought.

Bakan's suggestions for reforming corporations are intriguing and varied. He suggests, for instance, that social responsibility could be written into the charters of corporations. He is also a critic of the idea that governments can always aim for greater efficiency by outsourcing services to corporations – which makes sense, given that any improvements in efficiency are most likely to be passed on in the form of profits to shareholders rather than returned to taxpayers.

Possibly some of his positive suggestions are utopian; however, they have the virtue of being rooted not in hardline ideology or an anti-capitalist stance but in legal experience and a pragmatic understanding of the obstacles. Given recent examples, from Enron to the global financial crisis, it seems likely that there will be many more corporate scandals and disasters in coming years, so it's possible that this book will come to be seen as prescient by readers of the future.

┌─ **THE SPEED READ** ─────────────────────────────

The Corporation

Corporations are essentially psychopaths – they have been granted the status of being a 'person' under US law and have a legal duty to put the pursuit of profit for their shareholders above all other interests. Bakan argues that we need to reform the fundamental legal basis of the corporation to make the world of business function with greater social responsibility and more sustainability in future. Based on interviews from across the political spectrum, this is a fascinating read that questions the very basics of corporate business behaviour in the world today.

Purple Cow

Transform Your Business by Being Remarkable

Seth Godin, 2003

Seth Godin is an internet entrepreneur and writer who has an entertaining way of framing fairly obvious business ideas so that they sound revolutionary. For example, at his online revenue-sharing, article-writing business Squidoo, articles were referred to as 'lenses' on the basis that they focused light and showed people what they needed to know. Like so many internet start-ups the company was eventually sold on to a larger conglomerate.

Godin's books are very readable, and frequently inspiring. *Purple Cow* can be seen as a bible for hipster start-ups so your attitude to it may depend on how you feel about organic coffee bars, ironic T-shirts, ethically sourced knitwear and the virtues of the 'sharing economy'. Beyond that, it is well worth reading if you have limited marketing experience, as it is a valuable insight into the approach and mentality required to hype, market, network and 'feed the buzz' in today's complicated world in which social media saturates everything and sophisticated consumers are sceptical of traditional advertising methods.

The basic pitch of the book is that companies can no longer rely on the traditional methods of pricing, publicity and promotion and now require something more spectacular to break out from the crowd. The something special that they need is the 'Purple Cow' of the title – something so unexpected, remarkable and thrilling that it grabs people's attention. You then market this purple cow directly to the people who are most influential and most likely to pass on the idea – Godin charmingly refers to such people as 'sneezers', as they are the people who will spread the virus of this idea.

As part of his own marketing Godin sent out early copies of the book in milk cartons printed up with his attractive purple cow logo. He also sold the initial print run of the book at a relatively cheap price, but you had to buy twelve copies at a time. The plan was that the sneezers would snap up the offer and then pass on copies to other people. Godin was already a well-known internet guru at this stage, so he had an advantage, but it has to be admitted that his marketing for the book was brilliant and a good advertisement for his own claims.

The plan is to create a remarkable product in a category in which people are already willing to buy, focus on early adopters, make it simple for them to spread the word and then let the product work its way into the mass market from that point. Godin is somewhat contemptuous of traditional marketing and advertising methods, referring condescendingly to the 'TV-industrial complex', by which he means the advertisers who have come before him who used old-fashioned techniques.

This is a pointer to a weakness in Godin's writing. He is dismissive of any marketing advice other than his own and too easily characterises all other approaches as bunkum. He misses the fact that companies large and small have always relied to some degree on the kinds of direct marketing he is describing and that (for instance) television advertising is more often used by large companies to maintain market share for their products than as the sole channel for new product launches. These have always relied as much on getting the product to key influencers as on blanket publicity. In addition, by dismissing the possibility of appealing to the mass audience that is reached by the dreaded TV-industrial complex, one could argue that Godin is only talking about launching products that will appeal to the young, hip audience of consumers who are still willing to try something radical. He forgets that this is not the entire marketplace.

From the very start, when Godin claims traditional business was all about pricing, promotion and publicity, some old hands in the marketing trade will be shaking their heads, thinking that here is a young whippersnapper who thinks he has reinvented the wheel. Of course, the world of the internet and social media has radically transformed how people interact with companies and each other. But it is fair to point out that Godin's message is not nearly as revolutionary as he would like to think.

Having said that, this is still a recommended read. Godin writes with an evangelistic sense of fun that carries the reader through the bite-sized chunks of chapters. He is funny, charming and makes many valuable, detailed points about how messages are transmitted and received in the marketplace. And if you don't have much marketing experience but have a great idea for a business, then this would be the perfect place to start. Godin will give you inspiration and enthusiasm in bucketloads and is likely to inspire good marketing ideas (so long as you don't get too carried away with the milk cartons).

Purple Cow

The old ways of marketing are uncool and useless and it is no use trying to launch a new product via the 'TV-industrial complex' any more. Pricing, promotion and publicity aren't enough in an age of social media and jaded consumers. Instead you need to come up with a product that hip people want, find the real influencers (or 'sneezers') and then show them your 'purple cow', something so extraordinary and attention-grabbing that they can't help but want to pass the idea on. Soon the world will be full of purple cow tattoos, ironic purple cow T-shirts, ethically sourced, purple cow knitwear and . . . you get the picture.

The Smartest Guys in the Room

The Amazing Rise and
Scandalous Fall of Enron

Bethany McLean and Peter Elkind, 2003

Timing can be everything when it comes to books about business. In 2000, *Leading the Revolution* by corporate guru Gary Hamel was published. In many respects it was a fascinating read, arguing that companies of the twenty-first century needed to take truly revolutionary approaches to being the best in the world. However, it was either very unfortunate or very wrong-headed in that one of the companies that Hamel lauded as being brilliant at what they did was Enron, the corporation that spent the bulk of the time for which the first edition of the book was on the bookstore shelves starting its slow, painful implosion.

Hamel's book is still worth a read, especially in the later, revised editions, but for the real dirt on the Enron story, a far better bet is *The Smartest Guys in the Room.* Bethany McLean was a young writer for *Fortune* who took a look at Enron in 2001, when it was widely regarded as the epitome of a modern, well-run company. Indeed it had recently been named 'most innovative large company' in the USA in *Fortune's* Most Admired Companies survey.

Prompted by concerns that a financial analyst had shared with her, McLean wrote an article asking a surprisingly simple question: how exactly was Enron making its money? She suggested that the company might be overvalued, given the evidence she could see of their activities and that investors and Wall Street analysts couldn't answer to the question of why Enron's share price kept increasing, to a high of over $90 in 2000. In the financial records she had noted 'strange transactions', 'huge debt' and 'erratic cash flows'.

Of course, we now know that Enron was in huge trouble that had been concealed over the course of several years by nonsensical accounting techniques, mark-to-market valuations of dubious assets and other shenanigans. But it was brave for McLean to make this point when she did. She was, however, soon vindicated, as Enron's share price crashed to less than a dollar through 2001 – by December they had become the biggest corporation to declare bankruptcy in American history (at the time).

McLean subsequently wrote *The Smartest Guys in the Room* with Peter Elkind, an investigative journalist who wrote for the *New York Times* and the *Washington Post*. It remains the best book on the Enron scandal, both detailed and exhaustively researched while funny and revealing. (It can be read in conjunction with *Power Failure* by Sherron Watkins and Mimi Swartz, which gives Watkins' insider's view of how so many Enron executives refused to see what was going on.)

The authors are good at explaining the financial chicanery that was being pushed by senior figures in the company such as Jeff Skilling and Andy Fastow (and ignored by CEO Ken Lay), including peculiar uses of the monetisation of assets, securitisation and so on. In particular, the way that shell companies were used, owned less than 50 per cent by Enron itself, that could buy assets from the parent company at whatever fantasy price was required, is well explained.

The role of accountancy firms and auditors in waving through the dubious corporate finance is also detailed. In one hilarious passage it is explained that you might have a dog, when the company needs you to have a duck. So all you need to do is paint the dog white and yellow, stick an orange beak on its nose and say to your accountants, 'This is a duck, right?' To which the accountants would reply, 'Of course it's a duck, since it complies with the rules that define what a duck is.' It is this refusal to acknowledge reality and to distinguish what is ethical from what is legal that underpins so many bad business practices. (It is arguable whether there has been real change in this respect in the intervening years – the accountancy firm Arthur Andersen suffered a serious decline as a result of its role in Enron, but many doubt that wider practises have really changed sufficiently to prevent another Enron in the future.)

Based on hundreds of original documents and interviews, this is a morality tale about sharp practice, greed and deception and, in particular, the dangers of groupthink. There were individuals at Enron who questioned what was going on but they were ignored, mocked or ostracised and the truth remained buried until it was too late.

Sometimes company solidarity is a virtue, but when it strays across the line into blind loyalty it can also be one of the most dangerous of vices, as this book lays bare.

The Smartest Guys in the Room

The story of the dizzying rise and abrupt collapse of Enron, told by investigative journalists Bethany McLean, whose 2001 article in *Fortune* asking whether the company was overvalued was one of the canaries in the coalmine of the disaster, and Peter Elkind. A forensic examination of how foolishness, sharp practices, self-deception and dubious ethics led to one of the most spectacular company failures in history.

Never Eat Alone

And Other Secrets to Success, One Relationship at a Time

Keith Ferrazzi, 2005

According to Ferrazzi, the secret to success lies in the relationships you form with other people. He argues that most successful people are good at connecting with others. If you take two equally talented people, the one who is better at forming relationships with others will do the best. In this book, he shares his secrets for connecting with others and making those connections mutually beneficial in order to help you achieve your goals.

For Ferrazzi, networking is about more than just professional interests: indeed, it seems to embody his entire life. He argues that you shouldn't compartmentalise your life into personal and business: they should be part of the same world. Dinner parties and opportunities to socialise – even getting involved in local organisations should all be seen as a way of developing your connections in a way that will eventually benefit you. He rejects the standard notion of networking (collecting a list of contacts that are seen as assets to you), in favour of a more mutually beneficial approach and makes the distinction between genuine relationship building and 'glad-handing'. But however much he claims that his way of connecting to the world around him is based on generosity (by helping friends connect with others, or doing something to help someone who might eventually help you), it isn't hard to feel exhausted by his sheer insistence that each time you are thrown into a social situation whether by choice or obligation, you should see it as an opportunity to make connections.

He does point out that forming genuine relationships involves being interested in the other person and encouraging them to be interested in you, but it all feels a bit forced. This approach is all well and good but if, at the back of your mind, the purpose of helping someone is the chance of a beneficial reciprocation of your efforts, then can it possibly be as genuine as he makes out? The idea ultimately comes across as self-serving even though he does stress that you shouldn't 'keep score' (in other words, keep tabs on who has done what for who).

Through the four sections of this book you are taught to become a member of the club to which you want to belong by joining relevant interest groups and taking courses while defining your mission and starting to collect those contacts before you really need them. You are never just making friends. Indeed, according to Ferrazzi, you should be quite upfront about what you want to achieve when connecting with these people, while avoiding being a 'network jerk'.

Section two covers the necessary skill set required for this task, which is mostly about researching the people you want to connect with and then getting their contact details. You are told to follow up these contacts, keep refreshing them and always use social events like dinner parties or meals in restaurants to further those connections by inviting these people into your personal life. You should even try inviting them to share your passions (whether that is art, golf, theatre, politics or whatever). All in the cause of building stronger relationships. He's not really talking about making friends though – there's always an ulterior motive behind every connection he makes and this is what makes this book so uncomfortable to read.

The next section deals with turning your connections into lifetime supporters and using an interest in their personal life to keep them onside. He adopts the IT term 'pinging' to describe constantly checking in with your contacts to keep the connection alive. (He also refers to the breakdown of his previous relationship. He clearly wasn't doing enough 'pinging' in that department.)

In section four the reader is told to build their brand by being 'interesting' so that people want to know them and to broadcast their brand by letting as many people as possible know what image they are trying to cultivate.

A final warning: after reading this book you will never be able to have a conversation with a stranger in a social situation in the same way ever again. This might be because you are religiously following his advice and treating the meeting as a networking opportunity or it may be that you will just be bogged down by the suspicion that the person you are talking to is the one who is following his advice.

Utterly exhausting and utterly depressing.

Never Eat Alone

Don't make a to-do list, make a to-meet list. Do your research on the people you want to meet. Make genuine connections, don't just collect people as assets. Be useful to them in the hope they will one day be useful to you but don't keep score. Don't separate the private and professional sphere: instead, invite your contacts into your social life and share your passions with them. Keep in touch with them and keep being helpful. All these connections are a way to continue making progress towards your goal. If you meet someone who you can't help and who can't help you, ignore them, they're useless to you.

Nice Girls Don't Get the Corner Office

Unconscious Mistakes Women Make
That Sabotage Their Careers
Lois P. Frankel, 2004

This book lists 101 mistakes that women make in the business world that executive coach Dr Lois Frankel sees as
being directly related to how women are socialised in society
and how they consequently perceive themselves. The book
carries throughout the message that women do not have to
act the way they were taught to.

Frankel believes that little girls learn early in life that
success is dependent on being 'nice' but argues that this does
not translate successfully into an office environment. The
subtle stereotyped behaviours that women have internalised
contribute to creating the impression that women are less
competent. Although perhaps a bit reductive and generalised
on the subject of how women behave, the book nonetheless
contains some interesting points that could be useful for
women aiming for workplace success.

The book starts with a self-assessment for readers in order
to establish how true certain statements are in relation to
their own behaviour. Female readers are supposed to use this
to identify their weaknesses and strengths and to create a

personal development chart for becoming more successful. Frankel thus encourages acceptance from the start of the need to change your behaviour and perceptions.

The 101 mistakes are divided into seven categories. It would be too much in this summary to list all 101 so instead we will look at a few examples in each category. The first section is 'How You Play the Game'. Frankel argues that business is a game and you must learn the rules and play by them. She lists mistakes such as doing work for others (because it makes you appear subservient), waiting to be given what you want rather than asking for it, holding your tongue (because disagreeing doesn't equate with being disagreeable) and failing to professionally capitalise on relationships, preferring stable friends instead.

In the second section, 'How You Act', Frankel insists that women must change the way they think about leadership in order to change self-sabotaging behaviour. Mistakes include seeking acceptance or validation from others (which makes you seem unconfident), acting like a man, not standing up for yourself, feeding others (literally, because this makes you seem maternal rather than managerial), sharing too much personal information and being overly concerned with offending others.

'How You Think' concerns the reader's willingness to change and discusses mistakes such as viewing men in authority as father figures, accepting traditional roles, skipping meetings to which you don't feel you can contribute (because you should be there to prove you are interested in the business), letting others waste your time, explaining any setbacks by making up negative stories (like, 'He didn't like my presentation' or 'Maybe I wore the wrong dress') and prematurely abandoning career goals during employment gaps. These kinds of negative beliefs about yourself need to be disregarded in order to get ahead.

In 'How to Brand and Market Yourself' Frankel discusses the importance of seeing every professional as a product. The key to positioning yourself in the workplace is creating a product worth buying into. Mistakes include failing to identify your brand, being too modest, not having a sense of self-worth, staying in your safety zone instead of accepting challenges and being invisible rather than taking the initiative. Frankel also mentions the importance of using your full name in emails, business dealings, phone calls and introductions and advises never using a nickname. This probably sounds obvious but it can be argued that Frankel is referencing the 'need to be liked' aspect of female behaviour, when you can sometimes try to appear less formal in order to be seen as friendly and approachable. For her, this is a sure-fire way to lose authority.

'How You Sound' takes the premise that an idea has to be heard if it is ever to be recognised. Here the mistakes include asking permission rather than stating intentions, talking too fast, softly or at a high pitch, overapologising and using qualifiers (it weakens your message if you say things like, 'I sort of . . .', 'Perhaps I could . . .' or 'Maybe it would be better if . . .').

'How You Look' is the section that gets the most criticism from feminist reviewers; however, Frankel insists that appearance counts – whether you like it or not. She makes the old point that you should dress for the job you want, not the job you have (which could arguably apply to men as well as women). Mistakes in this respect include inappropriate clothing, make-up or having the wrong hairstyle, grooming in public and tilting your head when listening (because it looks girly and incompetent). In fairness, this probably is the most spurious chapter, since most women know how to dress appropriately for work and dressing for the job you want is not much use if you work as a receptionist but want to be a mountaineering guide.

The final section is 'How You Respond'. For Frankel, the way you react to others can signal your acceptance of their treatment of you. The mistakes include taking notes, getting coffee, making photocopies for others (unless this is actually part of your job), internalising messages, showing too much patience, putting the needs of others before your own, being the last to speak at a meeting, not being actively engaged and tolerating inappropriate behaviour or sexual harassment instead of standing up for yourself.

There is also a mini-section on the subject of women dragging other women down or not promoting them. This is often much ignored in business guides for women where it is usually male behaviour that is seen as the problem. Frankel rightly stresses the need for this to change in order to alter the workplace dynamic and allow more women to become successful.

THE SPEED READ

Nice Girls Don't Get the Corner Office

A guide to the most common mistakes women make in the workplace that can prevent them from fulfilling their potential, including advice such as:

- Learn how to play the game – *don't* . . . pretend it isn't a game, make excuses/do work/hold your tongue for others.

- Change the way you act – *don't* . . . try to be nice, flirt, acquiesce to bullies, feed others, share too much personal information.

- Change the way you think – *don't* . . . view men in authority as father figures, let people waste your time, abandon career goals, make up negative stories.

- Be aware of how you brand and market yourself – think of yourself as a brand or product, *don't* . . . wait to be noticed, be modest, stay in your safety zone, turn down big assignments, give away your ideas.

- Be aware of how you sound – *don't* . . . speak too softly, too high or too fast, use non-words, use hesitant language, fail to pause/reflect before answering a question.

- Make sure you look the part.

- Know how to respond to how others treat you – *don't* . . . internalise messages, tolerate inappropriate behaviour, let the mistakes of others inconvenience you, cry or allow yourself to be the scapegoat.

The Black Swan

The Impact of the Highly Improbable

Nassim Nicholas Taleb, 2007

There are many books that aren't strictly about business but that still have at least one idea that is important and relevant to business people. *The Black Swan* is an example – it is a long book that some find erudite, droll and brilliant, while others find overwritten, arrogant and pretentious. The core message of the book is that humans are not good at recognising or dealing logically with randomness, especially in situations in which variations can be great.

The title references the idea, long-held in Europe before the discovery of the species in Australia, that all swans were white. The 'black swan' was a byword for impossibility, until reports came back from the new continent that there were indeed black swans to be found. In the eighteenth century the philosopher David Hume referred to this in attacking the idea of 'induction', the suggestion that, simply because something has happened in the past, it will always happen. Not that induction is always invalid – we assume the sun will come up tomorrow because it always has and for the time being that assumption seems safe. But inductive conclusions can rarely be guaranteed and that is all the more the case when it comes to genuinely contingent facts.

Taleb uses the idea to refer to something that everyone thought was highly unlikely right up until it happened. Recent examples given in the book include the 9/11 attacks on New York and the rise of the internet (in particular, the astonishing success of Google in applying a business model that simply didn't exist a few years earlier). Shortly after the publication of the book, the collapse of the subprime mortgage market and the global financial crisis made the book seem extremely prescient, since this too was an event that most analysts regarded as highly improbable.

In statistical terms, we tend to see probability through the standard Gaussian model of the bell curve and to assume that events at the far ends of the curve are all but impossible, when they might just be rare or even inevitable (in the case of the subprime crisis). And the danger is that we look back and, with hindsight, find explanations which make us forget the irrationality that led us to assume that the worst would never happen.

Investors may find Taleb's thoughts on his 'barbell' method of investment interesting. The barbell basically involves placing most of your bets on the safest investments, apart from some 10–15 per cent which goes on highly speculative gambles, on the assumption that a few of these may well come good.

Beyond that, for business people, Taleb's moral isn't that we should attempt to predict black-swan events. It is that we need to allow for all possibilities and thus make sure that our business model has a degree of robustness built into it, meaning that we are not exposed to catastrophe in the event of a negative black swan event, but are able to benefit from a positive one.

This is not always an easy thing to do, of course, but we

can imagine an extreme scenario that would be very damaging or beneficial. One example is the impact of government regulation – if a heavy sales tax or international trade tariff were placed on your best-selling product as of next week, would you be in a position to cope with the fallout? If there is an extreme winter and sales collapse as a result, is your business robust enough to make it through to spring?

Good business owners ask themselves these questions anyway, but *The Black Swan* is a valuable reminder that it should be standard practice. Whether you read the whole book or just ponder the fact that induction from the past is an unreliable way to predict the future, you could help either to protect your business from harm and/or put it in a position to prosper when the apparently unlikely does come to pass.

Taleb points out that some black swan events depend on the observer – to a turkey living happily on a farm, the Christmas slaughter seems unpredictable, but it is entirely predictable from the point of view of the butcher. (Similarly a new sales tax may be a surprise to a widget manufacturer, but entirely predictable to the government officials who have been working on the proposal for months.) Taleb's metaphorical advice is to avoid being the turkey and try to get into the position where you 'turn the black swans white'.

┌─ **THE SPEED READ** ─────────────────────────────┐

The Black Swan

Humans are not very good at understanding randomness and can be taken by surprise by 'black swan' events – when something that seemed incredibly unlikely happens. Afterwards we can find explanations for such events, even when they were completely random. For business people, the moral is to consider the impossible or improbable and make sure your business is robust enough to survive a negative black swan event and, ideally, in good shape to benefit from a positive one.

└──┘

True North

Discover Your Authentic Leadership

Bill George with Peter Sims, 2007

A lot of books on business leadership and management tend to be self-regarding or bombastic, or to advocate Machiavellian or plain lazy approaches. (Yes, we do mean you, *One Minute Manager*). Too often, they proceed on the assumption that there is a set of qualities that make a 'great leader' and that you can learn either to have these qualities or, more likely, to pretend to have them.

So this book makes a refreshing change in that it takes a very different path. Based on more than a hundred interviews with a wide variety of successful business leaders and written by the ex-CEO of medical giant Medtronic, Bill George, together with Peter Sims, it instead focuses on each person's personal journey and on how to find your own way of being a leader, being true to your own principles and values. The authors go out of their way to point out that there is 'no such thing as the instant leader', in spite of the many business manuals which pretend that there is. (Yes, we do still mean you, *One Minute Manager* . . .)

The authors suggest that, along the road to becoming an authentic leader, you need to ask yourself three questions:

'Who am I?', 'Why do I do the things I do?' and 'What are my aims and aspirations in my life in general?' The idea is that you find a way to do business that is wholly right for you as a person and in doing so you act with real integrity. Otherwise, how will you inspire and lead if you lack true self-awareness or are acting inauthentically from the start?

The book isn't devoid of gimmicks and schemes. There is a diagram to illustrate the personal compass that leads to your own personal 'true north' (meaning your true self). And there are lists of such things as the 'five dimensions of authentic leadership' (combining your purpose with passion, basing your work in solid values, leading from your heart, connecting with people and working with self-discipline in all things). Some critics of the book also feel that it has too strong a focus on anecdotes to explain how particular individuals came to find their own leadership style, and that the authors don't necessarily tell you how to do that for yourself.

However, some of the anecdotes are in themselves inspiring and interesting. And the book is also notable for taking a sensible approach to work/life balance, as it advocates rooting leadership values in family, the community and your personal life as well as in the organisation or company you happen to work for.

George is also very strong in advocating the idea that good leaders continue to have mentors as part of their support group and to engage with those mentors in a give-and-take analysis of what has gone right and wrong. Here he is underlining that anyone who is trying to be a leader is also a part of the group or community of people, rather than solely an authority figure.

The basic ideas in this book, that the best way to become a good leader is to be true to yourself and that it is often more important to serve the interests of other people rather than just your self-interest, are not especially revolutionary or startling. But in the crowd of business books that present quick fixes and short cuts to success, this is at least an honest attempt to lay out some basic principles as to how leadership actually works and this makes it a book that is easy to recommend.

THE SPEED READ

True North

True leadership can't be found overnight or by following a set of rules. It depends on self-awareness and on knowing truly who you are and what you want out of life. Leadership is also not something you do on your own – you are part of a community, you still need mentors and support groups. And you need a work/life balance so that your leadership is rooted in your entire life. If you can be honest with yourself, and root your leadership in solid values and self-discipline, then you may be on the road to becoming an authentic leader.

The 4-Hour Workweek

Escape 9–5, Live Anywhere and
Join the New Rich

Timothy Ferriss, 2007

If you've ever wondered how much time per week you would need to achieve any given task, then wonder no longer. If you want to have incredible sex, lose weight and become a 'superhuman', you can refer to *The 4-Hour Body* by Timothy Ferriss. If you want to become a top-class cook and to achieve mastery of your life outside of the kitchen, he handily explains how to do so in *The 4-Hour Chef*. And if you want to escape the rat race for ever and join the new rich then, by an astonishing coincidence, this will also take you only four hours a week, and Mr Ferriss has all the answers to all your questions in *The 4-Hour Workweek*.

In case it has crossed your mind that this author sounds like a bit of an opportunist, shame on you for your cynicism. His books are published by reputable publishing corporations who are seasoned experts at fact-checking and credential-testing and surely would never allow a book making dubious claims to part their hallowed doors.

OK, let's start again. This book is actually a pretty awful bit of huckstering that comes in the long tradition of books that make ludicrous promises, going back at least to *Think And Grow Rich,* and that claim to be able to teach you get-rich-quick techniques. Like *The One Minute Manager,* part of *The 4-Hour Workweek*'s success derives from creating the idea that you can not only do this, but it will be incredibly easy and take almost no time to achieve.

Ferriss advises those currently in nine-to-five jobs to abuse employers and colleagues by skiving as much as possible, trying to get your job done in the minimal amount of time, passing on or delegating as much as possible and using the time to start setting up your own business which will generate a passive, 'automatic' income. If this seems like pretty shabby advice, it's worth knowing that he also boasts about having won a martial-arts competition by taking advantage of a loophole in the rules that got him into an easier weight group. He also suggests outsourcing large parts of your life in return for low pay to remote assistants in India and wasting your friends' time by asking them to provide you with information that you are too lazy to seek out yourself.

The aim of all this is to get yourself into a position where you only have to work a few hours a week and can take endless holidays in fabulous places to impress your friends (if you still have any at that stage) or repeated semi-retirements in cheap areas of the world. But the advice given on what business you can set up to achieve this is pretty nebulous and unconvincing, relying heavily on ideas like buying up Google adwords or setting up an online retail business with sufficient mark-ups to make fantastic profits. You would probably get as much genuine information out of a spam email from a member of the Transylvanian royal family who wants to help you set up a million-dollar business but just needs a few bank details first.

To be fair, along the way you might pick up the odd inspirational point about streamlining your life and trying to make your business work as effectively as possible so it doesn't consume your every waking moment. It may indeed be possible for us all to work less in the future, although one suspects that if everyone else was working four hours a week, Ferriss would still be that free-rider trying to get away with one hour.

Of course, it is a perfectly reasonable aspiration to reduce the amount of time you spend working or to create a business that allows you to control your own time. This would be at least part of the motivation for many entrepreneurs, although for the most part people want to create businesses that they actually enjoy, rather than fobbing off all the work onto other people and going on permanent holiday.

In the final analysis, Ferriss's best get-rich-quick idea is probably the one he doesn't mention in the book – put together a shoddy business manual with a flashy, attention-grabbing concept and persuade a reputable publisher to take it on, work really hard promoting it on social media, through blogs and so on until you have a best-seller, then repeat the formula ad nauseum using the same '4-Hour' tagline.

Perhaps he can stick that in his next book and call it *The 4-Hour Business Guru.*

The 4-Hour Workweek

Life's short and you don't want to spend it all being a sucker working hard at a nine-to-five job. So start now: either quit the job or just don't bother doing it properly while you take advantage of all the other suckers' hard work. Set up a business that will automatically make you loads of money, then swan around the world sneering at all the suckers who aren't as smart as you. It worked for me, so clearly it can work for you. (Not everyone else though, because there'll still have to be some suckers doing all the hard work.)

Ask For It

How Women Can Use the Power of Negotiation to Get What They Really Want

Linda Babcock and Sara Laschever, 2008

Ask For It is the follow-up book to *Women Don't Ask – The High Cost of Avoiding Negotiation*. Previously published in 2003 by Babcock and Laschever, *Women Don't Ask* explored uncomfortable truths around gender and negotiation and outlined the obstacles that so often prevent women from negotiating as successfully for themselves as men seem to be able to. The book explained how social and cultural conditioning cause gendered differences in the workplace and produce huge economic costs to women over the course of their working life. They said that as women tend not to negotiate their salary (in particular for their first job) and men do tend to, women can be paid $500,000 less over the course of their working life than men.

Ask For It builds on the success of the first book by providing a more structured and practical approach for women to negotiate in the workplace. Babcock and Laschever wrote it in response to the women who contacted them after the publication of their first book and following further research into women in the workplace. It is a practical guide for women to reframe their interactions both at work and in their personal lives. To this end the authors formulate a programme in four stages, each of which comes with exercises to prepare and succeed in any of life's negotiations.

In phase one, Babcock and Laschever tell women that everything is negotiable. They recognise that much of society's bias towards women in the workplace is institutionalised and can be internalised by women themselves. Readers are urged to ask questions of themselves to identify their personal and professional goals. Questions such as, 'What is your ideal job?' or 'When were you happiest in your work or at home?' go beyond the workplace and ask women to concentrate on their wider beliefs and attitudes. Phase two involves preparing the groundwork for negotiation. It looks at the skills and concepts of basic negotiating strategy, explaining that the most important thing is knowledge – of yourself and of how your self-worth affects your behaviour. They suggest looking online at what other people (men and women) are paid for doing the same job, listing your own achievements both professionally and personally and writing down your own long-term view of what you want to be and to accomplish. Also, try to find out things about the person you are negotiating with, as this information can be helpful. For the authors, this is key to negotiating, as being armed with the facts strengthens your bargaining position.

Phase three (with the title 'Get Ready') urges women to reach as high as possible when negotiating. They discuss the virtues of co-operative bargaining when making your first offer, ascertaining your worth and using trade-offs to get past obstacles and build on your value. There is even a section called the 'Negotiation Gym' with a six-week programme designed to help women through increasingly difficult negotiations to develop stamina and confidence in the process. This section aims to increase the power of women when negotiating to help develop a sense of having the right to be asking for something and to do the asking without seeming apologetic or self-deprecating.

The final phase is intended to show women how they can 'Put It All Together'. Babcock and Laschever advocate role-playing with a friend before any negotiation and to avoid making concessions too quickly when trying to get what you want. They also stress the importance of making the right impression in order to influence the person you are negotiating with and give advice on how to close the deal.

Like many books on women and the workplace, *Ask For It* has been criticised for being too focused on white, female professionals and not taking sufficient account of other inequalities such as race and background. Although there is substantial research into the subtle ways in which the social conditioning of both men and women (including that of women towards themselves) affect the status and achievements of women, there is an assumption that all women begin at the same level with the same disadvantages. This is clearly not the case and the book covers only white-collar jobs.

The book has also been criticised for taking a slightly patronising view of women who don't ask and therefore don't get, blaming them – rather than the structure of the workplace – for their lack of achievement. For example, it doesn't address the underlying causes of the gender pay gap. It also contains some contradictions, for instance arguing that women are conditioned from childhood not to negotiate while at the same time acknowledging that women can face a sexist backlash for being too pushy when negotiating. And the authors' answer to not seeming too pushy is to be nice and more co-operative but at the same time to overcome the social conditioning that says women have to be nice to be likeable and successful.

The book does contain some useful advice, especially on gathering knowledge and facts when negotiating and being prepared. However, it can at times be a little bewildering in the way it stresses the need for real social change while encouraging women to remember how society sees them, and in telling women to change their own ways to avoid the pitfalls of sexism rather than striving to change society itself.

THE SPEED READ

Ask For It

Get to know yourself and what you want – this may involve some soul-searching questions not related to the workplace. Everything in life is negotiable: you decide what is fair – run your own life. Learn to lay the groundwork for negotiation – know how much you're worth, learn about the person you are negotiating with (even little things can help). Get ready and aim high – refine your strategy and learn the power of co-operative bargaining. Pace yourself with increasingly difficult negotiations. Put it all together – have a role-play rehearsal for that important negotiation. Learn how to be likeable and how to close a deal.

What Got You Here Won't Get You There

How Successful People Become Even More Successful

Marshall Goldsmith, 2008

'Executive coach' Marshall Goldsmith describes the ways in which interpersonal habits that may have helped someone progress to a certain level in an industry may then start to hold them back. To this end, he lists twenty 'bad habits' that successful people can fall into which prevent them from progressing further in their chosen field. As the title suggests, it is primarily aimed at people who are already at management level and focuses on the traps they may have unwittingly fallen into that are holding them back.

Goldsmith argues that it may be more important to create a 'to-stop' list rather than a 'to-do' list. One crucial part of this is developing insight and, in particular, accepting that you need to be more aware of how your behaviours and actions are perceived by others. The author sees self-interest as one of the most important and potentially damaging traits that individuals at management level possess. He cites four main drivers: money, power, status and popularity. It is when we strive for these that we can develop unhelpful habits, which then become so ingrained that we're often unaware of them. And the higher you rise, the more likely you are to begin to display some of these behaviours.

One of the first habits that Goldsmith describes is the need to win at all costs. He advises asking whether this particular battle (if it is looking like a battle) is worth it. He stresses that it isn't important to always compete against others. The second habit is the need to add your own opinion whenever someone else offers theirs: he sees this as expressing an attitude of self-importance. Unsurprisingly, this can make you come across as overbearing and insensitive. Passing judgement is another faux pas: people in management roles can end up feeling the need to judge others constantly and, when this involves imposing our own standards on others, it can inhibit their productivity.

Many of the habits Goldsmith describes seem obviously sociopathic. It's disappointing that there are managers out there who need to be warned against making destructive comments, handing out needless sarcasm, always starting feedback with the words 'No' or 'But', being negative whenever someone else has an idea or failing to show gratitude when someone does something for them (experience would suggest that all of these behaviours are indeed quite widespread). In the same vein, he suggests that it is unwise to constantly tell everyone how good you are, fail to listen to others or to punish the messenger when things go wrong.

One good bit of advice is to communicate more with colleagues about what you are doing. If you don't tell people what is going on they can feel you are keeping them in the dark and this creates uncertainty and suspicion. His message here is to be more magnanimous in your approach to others, give credit where it's due, acknowledge your own mistakes and say 'Thank you' more often.

However, for every simple but obvious bit of good advice, there is another warning against obvious pieces of unpleasant behaviour, such as claiming credit for work that is not entirely yours or making excuses by claiming some behaviours are simply a character trait instead of taking a good look at yourself and trying to change. (At least Goldsmith's message here ends up becoming positive: that everyone can change their behaviour with a bit of thought and effort and that this change can be rewarding in many ways.)

In the end, much of Goldsmith's advice regarding the twenty bad habits boils down to checking yourself every time you behave like an arrogant idiot. Or at the very least examining your behaviour and trying to notice your own mistakes when you display these behaviours.

While it is a sad truth that many people in management roles display some or many of the self-defeating traits listed in Goldsmith's book, it tends to come across as twenty rules on how not to come across as a complete ********. If any one person displayed all the characteristics he lists, they would be unbearable whether inside or outside the office. It is true that having a managerial role tends to instil the need to display a sense of control and that may lead to some of the habits listed here. However, this is probably more use as a manual of what not to do for self-important idiots than as advice on how to overcome these habits and to move on to the next stage of success.

What Got You Here Won't Get You There

OK, so you may have reached management level and think you're a big shot, but it's time to accept that you don't know everything (and to know that some of the behaviour that got you this far may stop you from getting any further). You don't always need to have the last word. You don't need to always win. Remember to say 'Thank you' and give credit more often. Communicate what is going on to your colleagues. Don't think you have to pass judgement on everyone. Stop making excuses for yourself and acknowledge your mistakes. Don't cling to the past or claim faults are simply behavioural traits. And above all, remember that if you're a manager you're probably already a bit of a sociopath.

Ignore Everybody

And 39 Other Keys to Creativity

Hugh MacLeod, 2009

Hugh MacLeod is a marketer and illustrator, best known for his cartoons drawn on the backs of business cards. The origins of this book were in a set of forty keys to creativity he posted on his blog, Gaping Void, which went on to sell over a million copies as an ebook, before finally being published in print form.

It is obviously of most relevance to those working in creative professions, but it's also worth knowing that MacLeod sees the book as a collection of advice that he wishes he had received in his twenties. Those who have already been through the mill of creative work may find some of what he has to say a bit obvious, while those in the early stages of a creative career may well benefit.

It's a pithy book, decorated with MacLeod's cartoons. Its fundamental theme is the conflict between a purist approach to creative work and one that accepts that compromises will need to be made along the way. MacLeod talks of his 'Sex and Cash' theory, which is basically that some creative work is 'sexy' (as in impressive, satisfying, unusual), while some is more mundane but pays reasonably well. If you are lucky you may have work that is simultaneously sexy and well paid but most people will find it necessary to incorporate both sides of the equation into a career and the sooner you accept this inevitability, the sooner you will progress in life. At the same time it is important to understand that 'once your dreams become reality, they are no longer your dreams' – in other words, no matter how pure your creative aims are, success will bring plenty of hassles too. As the caption to one of MacLeod's cartoons runs: 'I do the work for free. I get paid to answer all the emails.'

The book is often rude and can be very funny, but it contains some genuinely good advice that carefully balances the purist urge with the need to make creative work pay. For instance, the suggestion that you 'sing in your own voice' and avoid crowded areas rather than attempting to stand out from the crowd are wise words for someone who is being tempted in the direction of compromising too much. And he emphasises that you are the person who is best placed to understand your ideas. The more original those ideas are, the less useful any advice from others will be.

There is some basic common sense about how difficult life can be for a young creative person. MacLeod advises frugality, hard work at all times and avoiding being tempted by the 'dying young' myth that glamorises drugs and alcohol. And he is scathing about the idea – held by too many young artists – that you simply need to have a brilliant idea and find a way to be 'discovered', writing that 'if your business plan involves being discovered by some big shot, your plan will probably fail'. Again, the aim isn't to put people off from a creative career but to emphasise the hard work and commitment and to underline the fact that you will need to take responsibility for your own work – and probably create the business plan for making money from that work.

At the same time he is good at explaining that 'selling out' isn't always the easy option and can still be rewarding in its own way. And he notes that selling out has its limits because, if you dilute an idea too far, it won't appeal to people in any case. At the same time he dismisses the idea that you can validly differentiate between 'artistic' and 'commercial' craft, which is one of the hang-ups people can have about finding ways to turn creativity into a business opportunity. And one of his forty keys is simply 'Keep the Day Job,' which may not be fun advice, but it is certainly sensible for most people.

Not everyone loves this book – some find it patronising or contradictory, some have dismissed it as the ramblings of someone who had a modestly successful cartooning career and was thus forced to 'sell out' himself by becoming a marketer. But for every one young creative who doesn't need to read this advice, there are probably fifty others who could benefit from hearing MacLeod's thoughts. And for anyone pondering the sacrifices and compromises that are usually required to move from creativity to a business opportunity, this is a light and entertaining but rewarding read.

THE SPEED READ

Ignore Everybody

A short, cartoon-based approach to the challenge of reconciling the pursuit of creativity with making a living. Forty pieces of short advice that will be most useful to young creative people who have yet to fully process some of the compromises and sacrifices they will need to make to survive. MacLeod briefly sums his own book up thus: 'Work hard. Keep at it. Live simply and quietly. Remain humble. Stay positive. Create your own luck. Be nice. Be polite.'[1]

---

[1] As quoted in 'Books of the Times: Greed Layered on Greed, Frosted with Recklessness', *New York Times*, 15 June 2009

Fool's Gold

How Unrestrained Greed Corrupted a Dream, Shattered Global Markets and Unleashed a Catastrophe

Gillian Tett, 2009

At the time of the global financial crisis of 2007–8, one of the most interesting writers on the subject was Gillian Tett, a financial journalist and specialist on the credit markets. She had been covering Japan when its financial bubble burst in the 1990s and her background in anthropology gave her a keen understanding of the tribal nature of the financial sector. Her book on the crisis was always going to be an interesting read.

She focuses on how credit derivatives and other financial instruments were invented and, in particular, how a team of quants at J. P. Morgan built a lucrative business out of selling them, following a decadent Florida corporate bash at which they discussed the concept while huge quantities of cocktails were consumed and managers were thrown into the pool. The Morgan team came up with the innovation of securitising not just loans but also credit derivatives. Many of the original team ended up moving on to other institutions and the practices they initiated became widespread. And, while they had not initially included subprime mortgages in the mix, that was to become the final straw in a disastrous edifice.

Tett can be a brilliant and acerbic commentator, but the biggest surprise about this book (and one of the most valid criticisms of it) is that she is not especially critical of the J. P. Morgan team, seeming almost to accept at face value their argument that the mathematical models and the derivatives themselves were not to blame for the crisis but the hideous mistakes that other institutions made when copying their business model. Her analysis isn't quite as simple as this, as we will see, but it is actually this flaw in the book that makes it so interesting from a business point of view.

If you allow Tett to put you in the shoes of the original traders, it's surprisingly easy to get caught up in the excitement of how remarkable a thing they thought they were doing. By spreading risk out so thinly, they felt they were abolishing one of banking's biggest obstacles – the danger that loans would not be repaid. And in achieving this they believed they were also unleashing the power of capitalism to create more growth as banks lent freely and used derivatives and securitisation to offset the risks involved.

Of course, with hindsight we know that this was a delusion and that spreading the risk out in this way simply meant that, when a high proportion of loans went unpaid or were defaulted on, the mathematical models failed (since they hadn't taken this possibility into account). What had once appeared to be a way of spreading risk turned out to be instead a method of concentrating it in one enormous default risk – and exacerbating the chances of that default by encouraging banks to lend more liberally to people at the highest chance of getting into trouble with repayments.

However, we all know that when businesses make mistakes big or small, hindsight can tell us what went wrong. And we also know that mistakes often grow out of enthusiasm for a new model or direction that seems so lucrative as to encourage us to dismiss or belittle the risks of failure.

Tett writes well about how it was frowned on even to doubt the efficacy of securitisation. She points to the many voices that did warn of trouble but that were ignored or ostracised as a result (and this is where her earlier enthusiasm for the J. P. Morgan point of view receives some due balance). Even in the early 1990s, experienced financier Felix Rohatyn had suggested that derivatives were 'financial hydrogen bombs built on personal computers by twenty-six-year-olds with MBAs'. And Tett acknowledges the way that the wealth and power that derived from the early financial success of this business model led to a kind of omerta within financial institutions about the possibility it might some day go wrong.

In addition, she describes the way in which, following the early evangelism of the quants, J. P. Morgan became instrumental in lobbying against tighter regulation of the derivatives market, another part of the chain of events that led to the crash. What could have been done to avoid the crash and what can be done to regulate against such disasters in future is uncertain, but it would be a brave writer who predicted that the problem has been solved when so many of the original players continue to be in positions of power within the financial industry while so little has been done to prevent a repetition of the crisis.

Written for publication in 2009, this book was something of a report from the front line and there are some inevitable weaknesses as a result. But on the whole it is a sobering account of what went wrong and valuable reading for anyone in a business where there is any possibility of groupthink (which is most businesses) – because it is often at the height of great success that the seeds of future failure are planted. If we can't recognise hubris and excessive greed at those moments, then the global financial crisis will not be the last time that such behaviour brings companies to their knees.

THE SPEED READ

Fool's Gold

Respected financial journalist Gillian Tett, writing in the immediate aftermath of the global financial crisis, tells the story of the J. P. Morgan team whose inventive approach to the derivatives market helped to create the conditions for the crash. While Tett is fairly kind to J. P. Morgan and lays a lot of blame at the door of those who adopted similar methods over subsequent years, she catches the insane optimism and self-confidence of the financial whiz-kids who believed they had all but abolished risk from the business of lending.

Drive

The Surprising Truth About
What Motivates Us

Daniel H. Pink, 2009

In *Drive*, Daniel H. Pink claims to have found a twenty-first century approach to the question of what motivates people. He argues that the old-fashioned way of rewarding productivity no longer applies in today's industries that rely more on creative and critical thinking than manufacture. He seems to focus on new technical industries when pitching his ideas, although he claims that his approach works just as well in education.

Pink identifies three main elements of motivation: autonomy, mastery and purpose. His argument is that instead of employing the carrot-and-stick approach (financial reward for results-based work), we should aim to encourage people to take a more creative approach to their work. This will give them a feeling of having more autonomy in their role and encourage them to perform better. Once staff have this feeling they will then have the third level of motivation – purpose. They will want to do better and do more purely because they feel that they are making their own choices rather than doing as they are told.

Pink is less interested in performance per se than in how people who do certain jobs think they could do them better. Apparently, being allowed to use their own initiative makes them more motivated than financial reward. He uses a lot of scientific jargon: for example, he distinguishes between 'algorithmic' tasks (following a series of predetermined steps or doing what you are told) and 'heuristic' tasks (allowing a more creative approach to things). This ties in with his argument that 'external' factors (financial gain) are less motivational than 'intrinsic' factors (feeling self-motivated and having creative control). He even uses the fact that monkeys seem to have an innate fondness for puzzle-solving as an example to support his argument.

This is all well and good in (for instance) an internet start-up run by friends, but he does ignore the fact that most companies need to produce some sort of results. It has become more common to give individual autonomy to employees in the workplace. And it has already been proven that giving people more control over their lives makes them more productive (presumably because they resent their job and boss less). However, people still need to be financially rewarded for their efforts and Pink is dangerously close to arguing that you can take the reward away, on the basis that it doesn't motivate people (this is certainly the interpretation that some critics have made of the book).

The idea that more autonomy equals greater happiness in an employee isn't a new one. The suggestion that there can be a more thorough trade-off between providing autonomy and financial reward is merely a short-sighted addition to what is already a well-documented approach to management.

Drive

Money doesn't motivate people. Abandon results-driven assessments. Allow people to be more autonomous and creative in their approach to what they do. Job satisfaction comes from enjoying the job, not from the pay packet. Monkeys make great employees, because they like to 'work' – in other words, they like to solve puzzles by thinking creatively and they will do it for peanuts (literally).

Start With Why

How Great Leaders Inspire
Everyone to Take Action
Simon Sinek, 2009

Start With Why moves away from most common business books in aiming to help people create a business built on customer loyalty rather than to assist in manipulating customers and employees. It is particularly relevant in today's climate of start-ups and mindful consumption, where the source of the goods sold can become an essential part of the company's story and a selling point.

For Sinek, it doesn't matter what you do in business, it matters why you do it. His book creates a framework for businesses to succeed beyond simply selling a product well. He uses examples of leaders from politics (Martin Luther King), to business (Steve Jobs), to pioneering (the Wright brothers) to illustrate how these people gained followers that created a brand out of a vision.

Sinek makes distinctions between the questions, 'What?', 'How?' and 'Why?' and argues that it is important to consider all three in business. 'What?' refers to the products and services that make money, 'How?' is the process of setting the business apart from others and 'Why?' is the reason the business exists in the first place. His thesis is that by letting people know the 'Why?', you create not just customers but loyal followers.

Start With Why identifies two ways of selling. The first involves selling through the idea of 'What?': for Sinek this always involves a degree of manipulation. Conversely, selling through 'Why?' inspires trust and this creates loyalty by engaging people's emotions.

He gives three ways of finding your 'Why?'. Firstly, look back and ask yourself, What was your original motivation or the specific problem you wanted to solve? Secondly, look outwards, ask a close friend why they want to spend time with you or consider why people are drawn to your business. Thirdly, look inwards: the best businesses have a bigger vision; this doesn't necessarily have to be philanthropic but it does need to inspire others. Once you find your 'Why?', let others know about it. Sinek argues that if you are true to your own vision, others who like it will follow.

It is a simple but effective message and one that is refreshingly different from those business books that appeal to pseudo-psychology in order to teach you how to convince people of your values (whether you have them or not). The message is that if people believe in you, they will buy from you. Many businesses, from craft beer to coffee houses to bigger companies, are currently following this model successfully. It could be criticised as an earnest quest for authenticity but the range of Sinek's examples gives his ideas depth and value. These are ideas that can be applied to large or small businesses, to the non-profit sector and to politics.

In short, don't manipulate; inspire.

Start With Why

A valuable manual for anyone who wants to build a business based on authenticity and genuine customer loyalty:

- What? – the products and services that make money.
- How? – the processes that set a business's practices apart from its competition.
- Why? – the motivation behind the business.
- Have a point of view about the world and spread it.
- Gain trust and loyalty from your customers by engaging with them rather than selling at them.
- A loyal following is better than a captive market.
- Be true to yourself.

The 10 Laws of
Enduring Success

Maria Bartiromo with
Catherine Whitney, 2010

Maria Bartiromo, then anchor for CNBC's financial programme *Closing Bell*, wrote this book as a collection of
personal tips on how to be a success, focusing on personal
attitude and inner resources rather than on dealing with
external factors. This approach leads her to discuss success
not just within business or material achievements but also in
all areas of endeavour (co-author Catherine Whitney is a
New York writer of many books on politics and business).

Bartiromo offers ten simple rules for success (which she
sums up in single words) and the book is easy to read and
straight to the point. The first rule is to have 'Self-knowledge'.
She recommends developing a strong sense of one's unique
abilities and aspirations. Without this, success isn't possible
– you need to be able to define yourself in order to know
what path your life will take and how you will pursue success.
Be inspired by others but accept that you can't be them. She
also stresses that success can be personal to you, not measured by someone else's achievements. This personal approach

is a refreshing step away from the 'how to beat the big boys' attitude that so many successful women take in books on business. It is also often as relevant to men as to women.

The second rule is to have 'Vision', with an emphasis on the need for focus in whatever project you are trying to make a success of. She advises against a scattergun approach to life and asks the reader to stay focused on what they want to achieve and then work out what they are going to do about it. This also relates to the third law: 'Initiative'. Basically, when you know what you want, don't procrastinate. Do something everyday that you would otherwise put off. This trains you to take opportunities when they arise.

The fourth law, 'Courage', directly leads on from 'Initiative' because obviously you need courage to make that phone call, take up that offer or pursue what you want. Bartiromo's advice is to focus on possibility rather than fear. See courage as an inner strength that enables you to overcome obstacles and take a chance when you have the opportunity.

Her fifth law is 'Integrity'. Bartiromo describes this as a 'gut feeling' when it comes to doing the right thing. This is what she believes will earn you most respect from others. It ties in with 'Self-knowledge' because integrity involves knowing what kind of person you are and acting in a way that is true to yourself. By having integrity you become more trustworthy to your colleagues and more likely to be offered opportunities. It also requires you to be yourself and act on your inner self-belief even if it means making yourself un-popular at times.

'Adaptability' is next on the list: Bartiromo views it as the opposite of complacency. The book was written in the after-math of the financial crash of 2008 and she refers to the need to accept change or job losses and accept that you will always have things to learn and that it is never too late to branch out if you want to keep things on track. This is sound advice for anyone wanting to switch careers or simply wanting to expand their horizons. In the current climate everyone certainly needs to be open to change.

The next law is 'Humility', which for Bartiromo involves understanding that you are not the centre of the universe. Don't be self-important. You need humility to see the truth about yourself and others and to have integrity and self-knowledge.

The final three laws, 'Endurance', 'Purpose' and 'Resilience' are again all linked. Endurance is required because success can be fleeting and you need to keep up the momentum. Bartiromo stresses the need to pace yourself and have the ability to sacrifice short-term gains for long-term results. To be happy you must look to the future and live life with purpose. A fulfilling life can transcend material factors such as income, job or status. And resilience is really just another aspect of endurance, because you must be able to take the ups and downs of life if you are to make a success of it.

With its emphasis on the personal, this book could be useful to people at all stages of life, whether already in business or just graduating and starting out. It focuses more on the self than other business manuals, but perhaps because of this stands the test of time better than many others. On the down side it doesn't offer much by way of practical advice as to how to handle specific situations in the workplace, especially for women.

The 10 Laws of Enduring Success

To succeed in life you need ten virtues:

- Self-knowledge – the ability to define yourself and what you want/are capable of.
- Vision – focus on what you are trying to achieve.
- Initiative – don't procrastinate, do something you don't feel like doing every day.
- Courage – gather your inner strength. Replace the idea of fear with that of possibility.
- Integrity – always try to do the right thing according to your gut feelings.
- Adaptability – don't be complacent. Accept you may have to learn and change.
- Humility – know yourself but don't think you're the centre of the universe.
- Endurance – sacrifice short-term gains for long-term results.
- Purpose – live life with a sense of purpose to be happy.
- Resilience – adapt to cope with life's ups and downs.

The Big Short

Inside the Doomsday Machine

Michael Lewis, 2010

There aren't many titles featured in this book which could be compared to a thriller, but Michael Lewis is such a superb writer and his subject here is gripping.

He takes a very different approach to the global financial crisis of 2008. Lewis does a good job of covering the basics of derivatives, CDOs, SIVs and other peculiar financial inventions, but his real topic here is the people who made huge profits and losses during the crisis. In particular, he focuses on the stories of those individuals who saw the crisis coming and, in some cases, gambled on the market crashing, by taking out short positions on the subprime mortgage market.

Those who predicted the crash include Meredith Whitney, the financial analyst who came to public attention with her bearish predictions about the future of Citigroup and other institutions; Steve Eisman, a contrarian money manager; Greg Lippman, a Deutsche Bank fund manager who advised investors to bet against the mortgage market; and Michael Burry, an ex-neurologist with Asperger's syndrome, whose company Scion Capital made huge profits from the crash.

On the other side of the coin, Lewis also profiles some of the biggest losers in the crash, such as Howie Hubler, a Morgan Stanley bond trader who lost $9 billion on the insurance he sold for triple-A rated mortgages, and Wing Chau, who created many of the CDO products on the market at Merrill Lynch.

The tension in the book arises from the fact that we meet these individuals long before the crash, at the point when those who ended up shorting the market started to suspect that there was something wrong. While most of the financial industry was going full steam ahead, sublimely unaware that there was any danger, Burry was scouring through documents to try to understand the fine detail of exactly what was being sold. Eisman was talking to traders across the industry and making trips to investigate exactly who these mortgages were being sold to (and concluding that a huge percentage of them were going to default).

It was not easy to take short positions – in some cases financial products had to be created especially for the purpose – and it seemed like an insane gamble to most observers. Many investors in the funds managed by Burry and Eisman lost all faith even as CDO indices started to plunge because the mark-to-market valuations of their short positions failed to respond as predicted.

Part of the reason for this is the role of the ratings agencies, which Lewis pillories mercilessly. Often underpaid and less qualified than those in the financial institutions they are supposed to police, the ratings agencies frequently had to have the products they were rating explained to them by the very people who had created them. It took a long time for them to accept that the whole edifice was flawed and on the way to collapsing like a house of cards.

Finally, we see the protagonists being proved right as the market starts to wobble and then to fall to the ground, even as seminars and meetings continued which were arguing the exact opposite: that risk had been abolished and the mathematical models that caused the crisis were flawless.

As a business book, the main value of this is in how clearly Lewis exposes the delusional groupthink that afflicted the financial industry in the run-up to the crisis, and how the contrarian, awkward intellects of those involved in the 'big short' had to keep faith in an idea that everyone was telling them was mad. Of course, betting on a financial crash can be seen as immoral, as Lewis acknowledges, and it can also be extremely dangerous. Many people also lost money even though they saw the crisis coming – they failed to realise, for instance, that it would take so long to arrive or that it would be so extreme that the banks would need to be rescued and near-zero interest rates and quantitative easing would be imposed. So it would be risky at best to look at the huge profits made by the people in this book and to try to emulate their approach.

Beyond business, this is simply a terrific story, as captured in the film adaptation (which compresses the details for the sake of narrative), full of fascinatingly eccentric characters, flawed heroes and as much schadenfraude as anyone could wish for at the cost of the firms and individuals who got the crisis wrong.

The Big Short

A ripping yarn about the global financial crisis, focusing on some of the biggest winners and losers from the collapse of the subprime mortgage market. A group of eccentric, contrarian people in the financial industry dared to think against the tide and to investigate how the market for derivatives, mortgage insurance, credit default swaps and so on was actually working on the ground. As a result, they concluded that a collapse was due – but the tension in the book arises from not knowing how long the crash would take to arrive and from the enormous costs they had to bear in the short term in order to make it through to the final pay-off. While the subject matter can seem amoral and cynical, we are also invited to recognise that the people betting against the crash were like the little boy who saw that the emperor had no clothes. They were brave enough to start shouting about it.

Steve Jobs

Walter Isaacson, 2011

We haven't included many biographies or autobiographies of business leaders in this collection. All too often they are hagiographic whitewashes or self-justifying twaddle. However, there are some that are definitely worth a read and this biography of Steve Jobs, written with his co-operation, is definitely one of them.

Jobs repeatedly asked Isaacson, who had previously written fine accounts of the lives of Albert Einstein and Benjamin Franklin, to write this book, before the author finally agreed (once Jobs' wife bluntly told him that her husband's cancer was likely to be fatal). Jobs gave a series of long interviews on his life, thoughts and methods in business over a two-year period and chose not to exercise any control over the final book (in spite of his usual fondness for the 'reality distortion field'). Isaacson also spoke to over a hundred friends and collaborators (not all of whom were fans). The result is a truly fascinating insight into an extraordinary life.

It is well known that Jobs was a difficult character in many respects and the book doesn't shy away from some of his more unpleasant traits, from his aversion to bathing in the early years of Apple and his complex reaction to feelings of abandonment in childhood, to his extreme levels of perfectionism (and the bullying and aggressive behaviour it sometimes led to). It is also revealing about his rivalry (sometimes hostile, often respectful) with his major rival Bill Gates, who often comes across as the guy you would rather spend time with out of the two great geniuses.

At the same time, we hear fascinating details about Jobs' approach to the task of building great computers (and other devices). We hear about his adoptive father, a craftsman who taught the young Steve to think about the beauty and skill that went into even the unseen parts of an appliance – this was the inspiration behind Jobs' insistence that even the internal parts of Apple Macs should be beautifully designed (and also behind some of the perfectionism that drove his colleagues to distraction at times). And Isaacson relates how Jobs saw himself as a bridge between the worlds of humanities and science, and the degree to which he brought a human element to the products he designed and combined measures of intellect and intuition in his work.

From a business point of view, there is much that can be learned from a figure like Jobs, even if we can't all match his perfectionism or genius. For instance, he talks about the importance of eliminating anything that is unnecessary in a product, of building a strong A-team and of making things that you all truly believe in. He also emphasises the need to debate, simplify and critique everything (to destruction, if need be) and reveals how he went about protecting and owning his own work.

Jobs doesn't always come across as an easy, nice or straightforward person, although we always have to balance this against a sense of awe at his intellect and achievements. After all, it is hard not to respect the man who helped to revolutionise home and tablet computing, digital publishing, phones and even animated movies (via his involvement in Pixar).

This is a book that could easily have gone unwritten and unpublished – Jobs had died by the time it came out, but many Apple insiders were unhappy with the content, and his wife reportedly refused to co-operate with the movie version of the story. We can't know what Jobs himself would have thought, but we can nonetheless be glad that he allowed this book to be written with a minimum of interference as there aren't many books that give such a genuine insight into a business pioneer of his stature.

THE SPEED READ

Steve Jobs

The unvarnished story of the creative genius behind Apple, casting light on his troubled childhood, his moments of inspiration, his tantrums, his unfortunate personal habits and much more. In particular it is the story of how his creations were the result of obsessive perfectionism and a relentless belief in what he was doing.

The Lean Startup

How Constant Innovation Creates
Radically Successful Businesses

Eric Ries, 2011

Entrepreneur and blogger Eric Ries, who has experience of both unsuccessful and successful start-ups, admits that he found it difficult to explain his success in writing. Indeed, much of the book seems a bit meandering and there is a lot of repetition of the author's favourite phrases. However, it will be of interest to those with a strong business idea for a start-up who don't want to put in too much financial risk and plan to begin in a basic way.

Ries defines a start-up as an organisation that is dedicated to creating something new under uncertain conditions. He depicts it as a tentative, 'Let's see what works' approach that does away with careful planning and allows you to just throw things out there and see what sticks. The approach seems current within today's climate of portfolio careers and frequent economic upheavals. His emphasis on adaptability will suit those who are prepared to fail at first but are willing to keep going until they succeed.

The first catchphrase that comes up (and which recurs regularly) in the book is 'Build–Measure–Learn'. Ries uses this to define a cyclical process: instead of creating an elaborate business plan for one idea he suggests being more agile, continuously testing your product and having the ability to adjust according to how well it is doing. If it is doing well, always ask 'Why?' When you've worked out what is creating the success, then you can start adapting it to make it even better. If it's not doing well you also need to ask 'Why?' Adapt and change ('Pivot or Persevere' is the instruction he uses here). The key to this adaptability is avoiding linear product development and becoming more agile and not being precious about the idea that you have. Once again, build a product and measure its success. If it fails, learn from it; if it's a success, learn what works best about it. Measure success in terms of value to the customer: if what you produce is beneficial to the customer then you are increasing the value of the product.

According to Ries, any business that is starting up has lots of things it will need to abandon before it becomes successful. His advice is to launch your company sooner rather than later because at this stage there won't be so much you will have to throw away. Here he uses another catchphrase, 'Minimum Viable Product', to sum up the approach he uses throughout the book. Start small, see if it grows and be prepared to let it go and move on to the next thing if you fail. Establish a baseline and always test your product on the riskiest assumption you can make. Only if the baseline looks secure can you build on it.

Ries suggests that it is better to measure your success by how many additional customers each one of your current customers brings in, not just to measure success by sales. You can be sure you're building a fanbase and this helps to get other people on board with your project. He lists 'Three

Engines of Growth' by which to measure your success: 'Sticky', a measure of how many customers you are acquiring; 'Viral', the number of additional customers each customer brings; and 'Paid', the amount each customer will spend. If all three are doing well you're onto a winner.

There's not much more to this book: most of the catchphrases above are repeated several times throughout in different contexts and there are plenty of diagrams saying the same thing to fill out the space. But at the heart of it there is a useful – if basic – message for those wanting to create a start-up: start small with few expectations and always prepare for the worst.

THE SPEED READ

The Lean Startup

All start-ups are in danger of failing, especially if they require a lot of initial capital. So start small and don't be too attached to one idea. 'Build–Measure–Learn' – and do this continuously. 'Pivot or Persevere' – be agile, adaptable and ready to change if something's not working. Constantly measure your growth by how much value the customer places on your product and see how many other customers they generate. Start as soon as possible; that way you'll have less to have to abandon. If it fails, rinse and repeat and aim for success the second or third time around.

Thinking Fast and Slow

Daniel Kahneman, 2011

Daniel Kahneman is a Nobel Prize-winner who has carried out decades of brilliant research into psychology and behavioural economics, mostly in collaboration with his colleague Amos Tversky, to whose memory this book is dedicated. The largest part of his psychological work focuses on cognitive biases and false beliefs and conclusions that humans are nevertheless prone to believing to be true. In the field of economics he uses psychological concepts of irrational thinking to challenge traditional utility theory, which treats consumers as rational agents, and suggests the alternative of prospect theory, which gives more accurate estimates of the value we will ascribe to goods and services, given our cognitive biases.

The basic thesis of the book is that, when faced with decisions or judgements we have two ways of thinking: 'System 1' and 'System 2' (not literally different systems, although that is a convenient way to talk about them). System 1 is the more instinctive, faster way to make decisions, often based on a very casual perusal of the evidence combined with gut feeling. System 2 is more considered and a slower attempt at rational evaluation. The bad news is that System 2 is hard work, so we instinctively tend to use System 1 and, secondly, that both systems tend to lead us to wrong answers.

An example of how System 1 gets things wrong is the 'Linda problem' – subjects in an experiment are told some details about a young woman who cares deeply about social problems and then asked to guess whether it is more likely that she is now 1) a bank teller or 2) a feminist bank teller. Most people give 2) as the answer in spite of the fact that basic logic would show us that all feminist bank tellers are bank tellers, so 1) must be the more probable answer. Effectively, System 1 has ignored the actual question and substituted an easier question ('Is it more likely that Linda is a feminist or a bank teller?'), rather than using System 2 to analyse the probability properly.

Another persistent cognitive bias about statistics comes in the 'Law of Small Numbers', which is our tendency to make sweeping judgements about a population based on a small sample. And this also holds in reverse: we expect a small section of a random group to reflect the statistical make-up of the whole. For instance, when asked to write down the results of an imaginary chain of six coin tosses (out of a chain of a hundred) most people will hypothesise a chain in which heads and tails come up equally often, whereas this will be less common than other combinations. Worryingly, even scientists who regularly use statistical methods are prone to errors of this sort and when asked to project the likelihood of the results of a small sample holding for the entire population, they will be far too confident.

One practical effect of this law is that we underestimate the role of luck and randomness in many situations. If a manager or trader has a succession of three good years, we will see this as proof that they will continue to be successful in the long-term, when it is far too small a sample for us to rule out the likelihood it was sheer luck. And this leads us to over-estimate the role of skill in success (and failure) in the business world in general. It has been argued that this is the cognitive bias at the root of the excessive bonus culture, which rewards short-term results handsomely and assumes that it is necessary to guarantee such results in future.

Similarly, most managers who have a successful period will come to believe extremely strongly in their own skill and talent and will only ascribe their performance to luck when a bad year comes along. This is an example of the optimism bias which gives us the illusion of having far more control over events than we actually do.

This leads to another error which will be familiar to many people in business: the planning bias. We overestimate benefits and underestimate costs of any particular endeavour. The example given is that in a given year Americans who replaced their kitchens projected that the costs would be $18,000, whereas they actually ended up being $38,000 on average. Many managers or business owners who have undertaken capital building projects or invested in new directions will wince in recognition at examples of this sort.

Kahneman writes brilliantly about these and many other cognitive biases: for instance, the anchoring effect (in which we tend to make an estimate close to the last figure mentioned), the availability bias (in which recent events affect our decision more than ones further in the past) and the focusing illusion (in which the thing that we are currently thinking about takes on a psychological importance out of proportion to its real importance). Occasionally, you might want to argue with the conclusions that the psychologists have drawn from a particular experiment, perhaps feeling that the subjects have essentially been tricked into looking more irrational than they are. On the whole, the evidence is inescapable – we make most of our decisions on the basis of fairly shaky guesswork and leaps of faith.

Reading about and recognising all of these biases can, in theory, help us to avoid making obvious mistakes in future (although it is clear from reading Kahneman how hard it is to apply this filter – he admits himself to many occasions on which he has made the very mistakes he has been studying for so long).

There is another good reason to read this book. Many other business and popular psychology books claim to be based in the kind of science which Kahneman is talking about. Reading this book will give you a far clearer understanding of the claims that are made about psychological processes in books such as *7 Habits* (see p. 80) or *Pitch Anything* (see p. 235), as well as titles we haven't included in this collection, from *Blink*[1] to *Nudge*[2]. Indeed, it could be argued that if you have read this one excellent book you will realise that you don't need to read those other books after all and can spend that time more profitably elsewhere.

---

[1] Malcom Gladwell, *Blink: The Power of Thinking Without Thinking*, Little, Brown, New York, 2005
[2] Richard H. Thaler and Cass R. Sunstein, *Nudge: Improving Decisions About Health, Wealth and Happiness*, Penguin, London, 2009

Thinking Fast and Slow

Humans are not as good as we like to think at making judgements or coming to decisions. We are subject to the optimism bias, the anchoring effect, the availability bias, misunderstanding the Law of Small Numbers and many other cognitive biases. When we think with 'System 1', we make quick decisions based on our gut feeling and are often wrong. If we make an extra effort and use the more rational and slow 'System 2', we do a bit better but still make mistakes. In the workplace, many managers have false ideas, believing that any good outcome is down to their skill and anything negative was bad luck or someone else's fault. When we set out on a major project we will almost always underestimate the likely costs and overestimate the benefits. Basically, people are really irrational and when we do something stupid, all we can do is try to slowly learn to be less stupid next time.

Pitch Anything

An Innovative Method for Presenting, Persuading, and Winning the Deal

Oren Klaff, 2011

Sometimes when you read a business book, you feel like keeping a checklist of all the most irritating gimmicks. In this example, that list would include: annoying acronym which won't help you remember anything (tick); spurious appeal to pseudoscience (tick); overpromising title that doesn't reflect the content (tick); untestable conclusions justified by appeal to genuine science (tick); confusing jargon (tick); and macho braggadocio (tick, tick and triple-tick . . .).

Klaff's book may claim to be a guide to pitching anything, but his experience and anecdotes are concentrated in a fairly specific environment – raising finance from venture capitalists and other wealthy types in *Dragon's Den*-type situations. He is somewhat disparaging about the US class system, which leaves a fairly narrow section of the population in control of such investments, while seeming simultaneously star-struck by the wealth and power on display.

The schtick here is that neuroscience plus a dash of macho posturing can help you to take control in pitching scenarios. He claims that you use your neocortex to make your pitch, which processes complex information in a rational manner, while your listeners are using the reptilian parts of their minds (or their 'croc brains') which basically means they are primarily working out whether you are a threat or not.

A large part of his recommended method is based on taking control of the situation. He clearly has experience of selling to companies such as Walmart, who like to make life difficult and demanding for you, as he writes well on the small indignities and disadvantages that are imposed on salespeople in these situations. One of his counter-proposals for this is to brag about your importance by starting out by telling your audience that you're glad you found time to meet with them, but will have to be brisk as you have extremely important appointments later. (One suspects this could cause serious irritation in some buyers or potential business contacts.)

He goes on to talk about how important it is to frame the situation in the right ways. His favourite cheesy acronym is STRONG which, without going into every detail, is basically a mnemonic for ways of setting up the story to appeal to your audience's emotions, giving them a hook and a prize to desire and finally getting a decision.

There are some useful points along the way, but he also does a lot of boasting about his brilliant techniques for controlling the framing and uses a lot of immediately forgettable jargon like 'four-frame, hot cognition stacking'. He also talks a lot about ways of playing frame games and becoming a frame master. What he doesn't do a lot of is help people to work out their own method for controlling or getting the best out of a meeting. His writing is clunky and he rarely offers a constructive suggestion where a boastful anecdote could fill the same space.

It may well be that people who are pitching to financiers in very similar environments to those with which the author is most familiar will find this a useful read. Perhaps the book should have been called *Pitch for Finance to Wealthy Investors*, although then it would presumably have had a smaller market. But it really doesn't teach the reader how to 'pitch anything' and its advice would be counterproductive in many situations. Not all buyers or investors attempt macho mind games – many prefer a genuinely collaborative process in which the salesperson works with them to find a mutually satisfactory solution. And many would feel personally affronted if you were to walk into a sales meeting and try to pull off some of Klaff's suggested sales gambits or, even worse, to use them to ask for a rise in your salary.

So approach this book with caution but if you happen to be working in a particular kind of macho, high-powered environment, you may find it useful in spite of its many intensely irritating qualities.

THE SPEED READ

Pitch Anything

I've raised loads of money from wealthy investors so I can teach you how to pitch absolutely anything to anyone. Remember when you are selling that the other side are basically reptiles, so you need to show them you are the alpha male and let them know how lucky they are to have you in the room in the first place. Then control those frames, pull those puppet strings and watch those monkeys dance to your ubermale tune. What could possibly go wrong?

We

How to Increase Performance and
Profits Through Full Engagement

Rudy Karsan and Kevin Kruse, 2011

This book is intended to be of use to both employers and employees, which is quite rare in the world of business books. The main premise is that employees must be fully engaged for an organisation to be at its productive best. The authors create a sort of road map that they believe will lead to this full engagement and raise questions that employees and employers should ask themselves through a series of activities and decision-making exercises designed to create an organisation of happier, more incentivised people.

The book opens with what the authors describe as the 'We' question. That is, when asked what their employer does, will the person giving the answer reply with 'We ... ' or 'They ... '? This, for Karsan and Kruse, is the answer that defines whether someone is fully engaged with the job they do or not. They identify three key factors that lead to full employee engagement: growth (employees will feel more engaged if they have career growth opportunities), recognition (being recognised for the good work they are doing) and trust (they must trust their senior management, colleagues and bosses).

The first part of the book looks at work/life balance in a historical context, pointing out that, before the Industrial Revolution, there was more of a blend. It was partly the dawn of factories and the idea of the forty-hour week which created modern working practices in which work and life are quite separate spheres. The authors argue that we now need to return back to the work/life blend if employees are to be fully engaged with the work they do. Getting to the 'We . . . ' mindset involves a person being satisfied in all areas of their life.

The authors suggest four factors that influence satisfaction: autonomy, utilising one's strengths, being able to learn new things and having control over how the job gets done. The idea that the more autonomy an individual has makes them happier at work is not a new one and has been covered by several other authors in the quest for a more productive workforce.

To create these conditions, it is not enough to be a great manager: the employee also has a critical role in getting an organisation to operate in this state of 'collective consciousness' that Karsan and Kruse describe. They argue that employees need to find their 'career bullseye', by imagining a Venn diagram where the three circles are passion (what they like doing), purpose (where they want to serve and contribute) and pay (the standard of living they choose) and finding that spot in the centre where there is satisfaction on all three levels.

The authors recognise that there is often an income-based relationship between employee and engagement but also argue that pay matters more to the lowest earners and that the relationship diminishes the higher up the income ladder one climbs. They advise employees to learn about themselves to know where they fit in, because this is where engagement will truly begin.

Towards the end of the book they tackle the issue of how management creates a vision of a harmonious workforce and focus on engagement (how to give the workforce pride and satisfaction in their work) and alignment (giving the workforce a clear purpose, using frequent two-way communication and making financial compensation based on quality of work). They argue that it is more costly to replace an employee than it is to re-engage a disengaged one.

Given that this book looks at an organisation from the point of view of both employers and employees, it seems more balanced than many 'goat-herding' management manuals and the way it moves the focus away from the idea of nine-to-five jobs is refreshing. The basic message is that a happy workforce is a more committed and therefore more productive one. As with many modern management manuals, the book also links to a website with tutorial videos and further exercises, and each chapter ends with a summary of the key points that makes it easy to digest. All in all, this is a recommended and interesting read.

┌─ THE SPEED READ ─────────────────────────────

We

A fully engaged workforce is a more productive one. Work should be blended with life rather than separate from it, so that employees can be fully integrated into the organisation. Employees should feel as if they are an important part of the organisation. We now live in a post-industrial world and roles should be changing to reflect this. Find your career/life bullseye at the intersection of passion, purpose and pay. Above all, remember that while job satisfaction may be important, so is life satisfaction.

The Wisdom of Failure

How to Learn the Tough Leadership Lessons Without Paying the Price

Laurence G. Weinzimmer and Jim McConoughey, 2012

The refreshing thing about this book is that rather than trying to invent a recipe for instant success, it acknowledges that failure is an important part of business life and is something we need to learn from.

Based on a wealth of academic research and interviews with many CEOs and other experienced business people, it focuses on the question of what they have learned from their own mistakes and from those of other people. Gerry Shaheen, a director of the Ford motor company, is quoted early in the book, saying that this ability is 'not only critical to successful leadership – it is genius'. The authors argue that our business culture tends to emphasise perfection and to focus on short-term goals (through the pernicious culture of targets and reviews) and instant gains rather than taking a more measured view. And they point out that this culture can make people fearful of trying new things or developing business models through trial and error, since the 'error' part of that equation will always be seen as failure. Thomas Edison once said, 'I haven't failed. I've just found ten thousand ways that won't work.' They wonder whether he would have been allowed to take such a view in today's high-pressure business environment.

The authors begin by comparing two CEOs who had similar careers up to a point. Both had successful academic careers and impeccable records and both achieved control of their companies after a period of widely acknowledged achievement. Of the two, Jim Owens of Caterpillar is still regarded as having been a successful businessman, whereas Ken Lay of Enron has become synonymous with the disaster that befell that company. Part of the reason for this was that Lay refused to learn from or even acknowledge some of the failures that started to afflict the business, preferring to let others brush them under the carpet through dubious accounting practices. As a result, the company was unable to recover and avoid catastrophe.

Beyond this introductory comparison, the structure of the book is relatively simple. Mistakes are grouped into three main categories: errors that stem from 'unbalanced orchestration' (problems of strategic use of resources); errors that stem from team dynamics (including bullying and poor communication); and errors that arise from personality issues, including self-absorption and hoarding influence and power.

The first category, of unbalanced orchestration, include over-commitment (for instance, the problems encountered when News Corp took over MySpace, or when LA Gear expanded into men's shoes), aimless drifting in new directions (for instance, the launch of New Coke) and putting efficiency before effectiveness. The latter is a particularly interesting section to read since it depicts situations in which companies become bogged down in trying to make their current business commitments work efficiently without ever stopping to ask, 'Are we doing the right things in the first place?'

The section on team dynamics focuses on problems such as passive-aggressive behaviours, trying to force staff to subscribe to a unity that they aren't feeling and excessive focus on internal competition. The examples include those encountered by business people as varied as Carly Fiorina of HP (heavily criticised for insisting on acquiring new corporate jets at the same time as laying off many employees), Mattel's Jill Barad (who resigned as CEO after a serious downturn in the company's results) and football coach Joe Paterno (who lost his job following alleged cover-ups in the Penn State child abuse scandal). In each case the authors look at specific mistakes that managers make as a result of self-aborption, micromanagement, excessive self-promotion, a tendency to hoard power or other personality traits.

There's no doubt that this book is worth reading for the anecdotes and some of the personal stories and reflections it contains. Business books that focus on failure are rare, and this one contains a wealth of detail on the subject (albeit focused on the USA). If there is a problem, it is that the advice on how to avoid mistakes ends up feeling a bit wishy-washy and even contradictory. As the authors acknowledge, what one manager perceives as 'empowering employees', another might view as being 'disengaged', yet the first quality is recommended while the second is criticised.

A leader who is too worried about bullying her colleagues may swing too far the other way and become excessively passive. A leader too worried about being focused on one issue may become too unfocused. At one point in the book, synergy is seen as a solution to the problem of 'roaming outside the box', but later on it becomes a potential error when it comes to staying focused on the right things.

As a result of this, the authors' final suggestions feel like a

Goldilocks-style scenario – if you're worried about what kind of porridge will make you a great leader, the answer is always 'not too hot, but not too cold'. They try to square this circle by claiming that 'moderation' is the key, but if you are reading this book expecting a simple answer to how to be a great leader, you may end up dissatisfied.

However, this lack of a one-size-fits-all solution could also be seen as one of the book's strengths. As writers with academic integrity, they naturally steer away from the excessive simplification and rules of many other business books, preferring a subtler, more complex approach. And if what you want from the book is examples of mistakes other companies and managers have made and to consider whether or not you or your company are making similar mistakes, this may be where the book's true value lies.

THE SPEED READ

The Wisdom of Failure

One paradox of leadership is that we learn more from failure than we do from success. You need to know what not to do as well as what to do in order to progress. The aim of this book is to present analysis of many mistakes made by businesses and individuals, so that we can learn and compare them to our own situation. At the same time it is important to understand that fear of failure can itself be a mistake – if we are too scared to fail, we may never try the things that would bring us the greatest success. This book won't give you a simple recipe for leadership or profit and at times the specific advice on how to avoid mistakes is not as helpful as one might hope for. But at the very least it will give you food for thought and may make it easier for us to talk openly about failures and about what we can learn from them in future.

So Good They Can't Ignore You

Why Skills Trump Passion in the
Quest for Work You Love

Cal Newport, 2012

This book promises to show you how to take control of your career (and therefore your life) by getting the skills to become good at something, which will lead to you getting rewards, which will lead to that something becoming your passion. Newport suggests four golden rules to follow if you want to love your job.

The first rule is not to follow your passion when finding your perfect career. It sounds a little counter-intuitive, but Newport argues that following your passion induces a lazy, selfish mindset where you end up expecting the world to offer you what you believe is the right job for you. Instead, you should aspire to do 'great work'. He suggests that this will be something that involves creativity, has a strong impact and puts you in control.

Closely related is rule number two: 'Be so good they can't ignore you.' The author argues that you should look for something that interests you enough for you to invest time and energy in becoming really good at it. This is likened to being a craftsman, in that you need to focus on what you can offer the world. You need to get rid of the thought processes that say that someone owes you a great career and accept that you need to earn it for yourself. He writes that you need to think of yourself as 'human capital' – see yourself as having marketable skills – and then decide which kind of capital market you are in.

A 'winner-takes-all' market involves continuously honing your skills in one particular area. An 'auction' market can take many forms of career capital from the various skills you develop. In the latter case you need to build up your skills so that you are admired for them and so become more highly valued. In this way you increase your capital market value.

Rule number three looks at the importance of control, for the sake of which you may have to turn down that promotion. Newport's argument is that if you take on too much too soon you will find your work will be unsustainable. You need to develop your existing skills until you are ready. There is motivational advice here: get outside of your comfort zone, stretch yourself and keep looking for ways in which you can expand your repertoire. Aim to extend beyond what you think are your capabilities and this will increase your capital value. Newport admits that when you try to gain more control over your work life your employer may try to thwart your efforts although he doesn't offer much advice as to how to overcome this, other than to aim to be so good that you can't be ignored any longer. He also recommends following the law of financial viability, meaning that if you think a certain pursuit will bring more control into your life, first look for evidence that people are willing to pay for it. If there is no evidence, abandon that route.

The final rule deals with the importance of mission and comes with the instruction to 'think big, act small'. Your pursuit of your optimum career capital (value), should involve small concrete 'experiments' in which you develop a skill, try it out and examine the feedback. If it is good, keep going; if not, change tactics. This way you gradually build up what you know works instead of losing everything on one large bid for recognition. Newport uses the phrase 'little bets', meaning that the way in which your ideas will be received will take the form of something like a lottery and some will inevitably fail. Your 'mission' involves marketing yourself well: you must get the recognition and encourage people to remark on your skills to get to that optimum career point where you are in control.

At that point you will have the author's three conditions for happiness: autonomy (feeling you are in control of your day and that your actions have significance to others), competence (being good at what you do) and relatedness (feeling connected to others). Simple, really.

At times this book reads like a fairly obvious careers manual, and some of the advice on what makes employees happy might be better off being addressed to employers rather than employees. The overall premise is that the more control you have over what you do, the happier and more engaged you will be. This is advice that reads like common sense most of the time but, in spite of the counter-intuituive suggestion that careers can't always be rooted in passion, there isn't much in here that won't already have occurred to someone who wasn't lucky enough to have got their dream job from the first day in the workplace.

THE SPEED READ

So Good They Can't Ignore You

Don't follow your passion when seeking your ideal job. Instead, look for things that interest you and invest time and energy developing skills in those areas. Focus on what you can offer the world. Accept the fact that you have to earn your ideal role. Turn down a promotion if you're not up to it. Market your skills in a small way at first, get recognition and gradually become remarkable. Be so good you can't be ignored.

The Power of Habit

Why We Do What We Do in Life and Business

Charles Duhigg, 2012

The Power of Habit is a detailed look at the science behind habit formation and in particular how they are established and how hard they are to break. Duhigg writes interestingly about psychological experiments such as those in which scientists measured brain activity in rats trying to find their way through a maze. Essentially, once the rats work out the maze, their brain processes are not so pronounced during future navigations of the same maze. The process has become habitual.

Duhigg presents this as an example of the way that the brain reduces unnecessary work – once an activity or thought process as been reduced to a habit, we need to devote far less mental energy to that process. The catch is that we find it harder to adapt the habit in future. Key bursts of mental energy are detected in the rats when they recognise the problem as one they have solved before and achieve the reward of a piece of a chocolate.

Similarly, humans also tend to turn many daily activities into habits. We recognise a particular cue for activity, we have a specific response to that cue and then we expect a particular reward at the end of the process. Duhigg claims that up to 40 per cent of our actions are driven by habit formation, which makes the subject hugely important.

This is a useful thing to understand in business for two reasons. Firstly, to adapt your own behaviour or to influence people you work with into changing theirs, you need to understand how habits are formed and changed. Secondly, corporations have developed the art of persuasion to a remarkable degree by employing psychologists and analysts whose main focus has to be on the way habits are formed in consumers of their products.

The book is divided into three main subject areas: personal habits, corporate habits and habits in society in general. In personal habits, the author looks at questions such as why some of us wake up for an early morning jog every day while others develop the habit of eating too many cookies at work. The essential message, which he repeats ad infinitum, is that to change or create a habit you need to aim for the right alignment of cue and reward. For instance, if you have a habit of going to fetch a cookie and it turns out that the trigger moment for this is when you are feeling bored, or have completed a mundane task at work, then you need to substitute a different 'reward' such as treating yourself to a little walk or a chat with colleagues. You first need to observe your own behaviour carefully to work out what the trigger actually is.

Duhigg repeats this fairly basic point, which is also one of the foundations of cognitive behavioural therapy, a few too many times. As with a few of the titles reviewed in this book, one can sense the pressure of having to deliver a book-length version of a proposal that is focused on one core idea. But it is an interesting and useful idea nonetheless and some of the detail he gives on how to change habits in one's own life is constructive.

The most interesting material is in the section on habits in the corporate world. For instance, he writes well about Alcoa, the company whose fortunes Paul O'Neill (who would later become the US's Secretary of the Treasury) transformed by focusing strongly on one main issue – safety procedures. This was an issue which both unions and management could agree was crucial – and along with instilling new habits, by teaching all employees specific safety procedures, came a general raising of performance across the workforce.

Of course, habits are also important to business from a different viewpoint, in that companies want consumers to develop a habit of purchasing and using their products. Duhigg analyses the difference between a product like toothpaste (which almost everyone uses regularly) and sunscreen (which people often forget). Fundamentally, this also comes down to the cue–response–reward cycle, as the clean feeling left by toothpaste is naturally rewarding. He also talks about the launch of Febreze, which executives originally marketed as a way of eliminating bad smells. The problem was that many people learn to live with odours such as the smell of their pets as they become used to them. After extensive market research, Procter & Gamble realised that the people who were using Febreze the most were instead using it at the end of a cleaning session as a final touch to make things smell good. So they marketed the product again, adding pleasant smells and emphasising this aspect of its use. Once it caught on they went back to marketing an odourless version that eliminated smells because consumers had by then developed the buying habit.

A few of Duhigg's interpretations of his anecdotes seem strained – in a section on gambling addiction, he seems to be blaming the gamblers and letting the betting industry off a bit too lightly (even though in other sections he notes how good companies have become at fostering habits in their customers). And his account of the Montgomery bus boycott in 1955 doesn't really feel like it is relevant, as it is more focused on the ways in which the movement spread and caught on. However, on the whole this is an interesting, if repetitive read, which has a lot to teach us about how habits affect our daily lives.

THE SPEED READ

The Power of Habit

Up to 40 per cent of our daily actions are the result of habit. Our brains reduce the amount of cognitive power needed for many repetitive tasks by learning a series of actions which become programmed and are extremely hard to change. If we want to change our personal habits – exercising regularly or cutting out unhealthy activities – we need to identify the cue which leads us to those actions and have the correct reward in place to reinforce the habit. Businesses can benefit from understanding habits – firstly, by instilling good habits in their staff and by understanding how powerful an influence these can have across the board and, secondly, by using marketing to persuade consumers to acquire the habit of purchasing and using their products, goods or services. In wider society, an understanding of how habit works can also help lawmakers, influencers and administrators to influence people towards good habits and away from bad ones.

Lean In
Women, Work and the Will to Lead
Sheryl Sandberg, 2013

Sheryl Sandberg, COO at Facebook, wrote *Lean In* as a guide for women who want to gain access to top roles in business. It is a relatively short book dealing with the problems women can face when trying to achieve and maintain leadership roles in areas that are still to this day mostly dominated by men. It examines why women's progress in this area appears to have stagnated, looking at the root causes as Sandberg sees them and offering solutions aimed at helping women to realise their true potential. (Men wishing to change workplace practice could also learn a thing or two.)

The first three chapters deal mainly with the personal attitudes of women; in particular, how they see themselves and the reasons why they may be holding themselves back. Sandberg points out that although there is no gender difference in attainment at school, men in the workplace tend to be promoted faster and rise higher. Sandberg puts this down to women having less ambition, meaning that men get faster promotion. There is also the assumption that men can combine a fulfilling career with a personal or family life, whereas for women this is still perceived as striving in conflicting roles, meaning there has to be some guilt in one or both of these areas for women.

Sandberg insists that women can thrive in the workplace and for her (perhaps rather patronisingly) the biggest barrier to achieving this is fear. Her list is quite long and includes fear of failure, not being liked, taking on too much and not being a good wife or mother. Her advice is to think, What would you do if you weren't afraid? (Presumably she is talking about advancing your career rather than smacking your manager round the head with a kettle.)

Sandberg recounts the story of a meeting involving a meal. The men took their food and sat at the table whereas the women tended to sit on the outlying chairs with their plates on their laps. When she invited them to sit at the table, the women declined. This demonstrates the way that women lack confidence in the workplace. Compared to men, women are more likely to attribute their success to luck, hard work or connections rather than innate skill, so they fear that they don't deserve their role. Her advice is that they should accept that they have earned it, even if they don't feel they have. (And, let's face it, you probably do deserve it more than the boss's ex-school chum who simply drinks in the right clubs and bars.)

Likeability is another theme in the book. Sandberg uses a study from 2003 in which a group of students were given the résumé of a real woman called Heidi – but for half of them the name had been changed to Harold. Tellingly, the simple name change produced hugely different attitudes from the students. Harold was seen as a likeable and more appealing colleague, whereas Heidi was seen as selfish and the idea of working with or for her was less inviting.

There are clearly societal assumptions made about men and women with the same achievements. This is an enduring cultural dilemma and, unfortunately, one for which Sandberg has no real resolution. She rightly points out the catch-22 this represents for women, namely that a 'nice' woman may not be seen as competent and a 'competent' one may not be perceived as nice. She recognises that the only way to truly break down this barrier is to fundamentally change the system, but in the meantime she advises women to stop being 'nice' and let go of the need to be liked if they want to succeed.

There has been a lot of feminist criticism of her willingness to conform in this way to enduringly male, competitive corporate values but she counteracts this by pointing out that, in her opinion, the fundamentals won't change until more women are in top jobs.

In the third chapter, Sandberg focuses on the fact that women can be more risk-averse and suggests that they need to overcome this because there is a correlation between risk and gain. In general, her advice here is to seek out opportunities yourself, ask for them if necessary, make yourself useful and show that you can do things flexibly. She advises women to avoid asking someone to mentor them and instead to find someone whose views of their efforts are positive, who can give good advice and supply vital support at crucial times. According to her, you should ask thoughtful questions, be mindful of this person's time (in other words, do not be too pushy) and gain their respect by demonstrating that you work hard and are good at what you do.

Sandberg stresses the importance of speaking the truth and being open about your personal life because your personal and professional life are not separate. She uses the personal example of having turned down a job in Washington DC because it was too painful (since her ex-husband lived there). A year later she contacted the same employer for a job and got it: in her view she was able to do this because of her honesty the first time round. (This seems a bit unscientific. It is most likely she got the job because of her accomplishments, and one can imagine other circumstances in which such honesty could have backfired.)

She also advises women against scaling back their career ambitions in anticipation that they might have a family. This can lead to them missing out on promotion because they don't seem interested enough or because of their own fear that they won't be able to cope in the future. Her advice is to keep the 'gas pedal' pressed down and not to let future personal plans prevent achievement in the here and now.

Sandberg also recommends that the parental role should be split fifty/fifty (she assumes that there are two parents at home). This is all very well but the real problem here is that most companies are not set up for or agreeable to the idea that the father is 50 per cent responsible for the parenting. Problems such as illness or school crises are still mostly regarded as the domain of the mother, even if she works the same hours as the father. Sandberg doesn't sufficiently acknowledge how much the workplace needs to change in order to make this fifty/fifty parenting responsibility a viable reality and fails to look at workplace attitudes to both mothers and fathers. She also rather incriminates herself by admitting she asks prospective female employees about their future plans regarding children to encourage, as she sees it, equality (but it's notable she only asks the women).

Too often, the status of a man with a newborn baby remains unchanged, while a woman with a newborn baby is seen as having an impediment to her productivity. Sandberg herself points out that people see her husband as a highly involved dad and don't see her as a particularly involved mother

– society still just expects it. She simply accepts this reality and suggests that doing things well is preferable to burning oneself out trying to do things perfectly.

In the concluding chapters, Sandberg begins to address the fundamental issues that prevent women from achieving the top jobs in the workplace and finally acknowledges that it is a structural or ideological problem rather than one brought about, or even soluble, by women themselves. She notes that it isn't necessarily a case of women versus men: women often don't promote other women out of a sense of self-preservation, to maintain their position as 'one of the boys'. She advocates a continuing dialogue on how the structure of working practice can be made more accommodating to women.

These chapters may begin to address those parts of corporate culture that many women find are the real impediments to success in the workplace, but the earlier sections have been criticised and rightly so, for reflecting the viewpoint of a privileged, white, well-educated woman. Sandberg, a Harvard graduate who was always near the top of her class, would be the first to admit that she comes from a relatively affluent, stable and loving background and that this helps. There have been many criticisms of her work based on class or race blindness. One book in particular, *Lean Out: The Struggle for Gender Equality in Tech and Start-up Culture*, edited by Elissa Shevinsky, takes on board these issues and is worth a read for its counterbalance.

THE SPEED READ

Lean In

Advice for women who want to reach the top jobs in business from Sheryl Sandberg of Facebook, including:

- Don't let your fear hold you back.
- Recognise your self-worth and feel you deserve your role.
- Don't try to be liked – strive to be good at what you do.
- Accept changing roles at work and adapt.
- Seek out support, but not in an obvious way.
- Be truthful with yourself and others: professional and personal need not be separate.
- Don't put future personal goals before your career opportunities.
- Aim for fifty/fifty parenting.
- You can't 'do it all' but you can do most of it well enough.
- Aim for true equality in the workplace and begin by talking about it.

Business for Punks

Break All the Rules – the BrewDog Way

James Watt, 2015

Throw away the rule book! We are the punk contingent and we're out to get what we want, our way, which is the DIY punk ethos. No corporate suits, business plans, market research – that stuff is for the boring androids in offices. This isn't a business with a product, this is a mission. Join us.

This is basically the message of *Business for Punks*, the graphically appealing book by BrewDog co-founder James Watt. He used £30,000 in 2007 to start a craft brewery company that currently has a turnover of around £30 million and has written a book about the way he did it. His own way. Not anyone else's. Yes, there is a lot of arrogance in the book, notably his dismissive attitude (and strong language) about anyone who works in even a remotely corporate environment or wears a suit, about other business books (boring!) and anything remotely conventional. He finishes each chapter with a quote from himself.

It is easy to read the book as a continuous boast about how good James Watt is at taking on the establishment and winning, what a rebel he is, how he was the first to do anything remotely like setting up a company without going down the conventional route of business plans and bank managers.

(Ignoring numerous predecessors, for instance Anita Roddick in the 1970s – see p. 125). However, the most interesting parts of the book do come from his specific, fresh approach to business. With the rise of independent start-ups this book seems quite relevant and it will especially appeal to the younger generation trying to make their way in a world dominated by globalisation.

That said, although he dismisses conventional business tactics he does stress the importance of finance and financial awareness even if this advice is wrapped up in his own hyperbole and 'spreadsheets can be punk too' jargon. He stresses the need to not overspend with company money and to proceed with caution where extra finance is required. He admits that he went on numerous finance and accounting courses before setting up his business (presumably they were run by boring suits but still gave him some sound advice) and researched his idea after discovering how popular craft beers were in the USA.

The initial funding for BrewDog was raised not through a bank but through a crowdfunding 'equity for punks' scheme. There have been criticisms that this was unethical but Watt has always insisted that his original funders saw a very healthy return on their investment. Indeed, he sees the company's funders as a dedicated community rather than abstract wallets, his customers as 'fans' rather than consumers and his business as a 'crusade' rather than a company. It is this different style of description that has allowed him to paint his business approach as unconventional while he still does the sensible things that all businesses must do to survive when it comes to finance, customer base, marketing and so on. In 2017 BrewDog sold 22 per cent to a not-very-punk private equity firm, which further increased the return earned by its original investors and further diluted the idea that theirs is a completely new way of doing business

Some of the less significant examples of alternative business practices given in the book can also be questioned. He gives an example of how, after BrewDog won a Best Beer award, the supermarket Tesco asked for 20,000 bottles a week to be delivered to their stores. BrewDog didn't have the bottles, capacity or money at the time but Watt got a £150,000 loan. He first asked his bank to loan him the money and when they said, 'No,' he went to another bank and claimed that the first had offered him a good deal but if this bank could better it BrewDog would move their entire business finances across to it. The bank came up with the goods. A good move but not so much outlaw business as common sense.

When it comes to promoting a brand, Watt advocates guerrilla marketing strategies. For instance, BrewDog had created a 55 per cent alcohol beer and they packaged a limited edition presented inside stuffed roadkill rodents, ensuring global news coverage of the resulting images. This one action put BrewDog on the world map: whether people thought it offensive or funny was not the point so much as the publicity. Similarly, naming a beer Punk IPA appealed to a sense of anarchy and freedom, creating a word-of-mouth buzz.

Calling your financiers your community and your customers your fans appeals to our tribal instincts; this makes the market not so much consumers as part of things. They feel they belong with this new trendy product and are part of the 'scene'. It all sounds new and exciting but one could argue that it is still just rephrasing existing truths. Even Watt's gung-ho approach to risk-taking falls a little flat when he adds: be extra careful with finances, study to learn what you need to know and know your market (including how to approach them to sell your product) – all these are basic business virtues. He is dismissive of conventional interview techniques and advises hiring people with a similar world view to your own rather then someone experienced in their field. Again, this is less radical than claimed – where several candidates for a role have the experience, the one who fits the company's ethos the closest is always the most likely to get the job.

This is a book that uses a lot of jargon to advocate a new DIY aesthetic as a business model and some of Watt's escapades are undoubtedly funny and take a lot of front and confidence. He has indeed been on a crusade, but it is difficult to tell whether this is actually business advice or a book about himself.

In conclusion, if you want to do business the punk way, don't read business books . . . except, of course, for this one.

THE SPEED READ

Business for Punks

A breathless account of the creation of the BrewDog brand and how to emulate it: remember, there are no rules, this is punk – go DIY. Don't start a business, go on a crusade. Learn everything you can about finance and accountancy while shouting you're not taking any advice because you're 'a bit of a rebel'. Don't waste money on marketing, just draw attention to yourself in whatever way you can. Call customers your 'fans' – they'll like it, it's very rock 'n' roll. Call financiers your 'community' then they'll feel like they belong with you and will show loyalty. Raise money however you can, don't just use bank managers. Finally, whatever you do, don't read business books.

The Idea in You

How to Find It, Build It and Change Your Life

Martin Amor and Alex Pellew, 2015

This is very unlike many other business books in that it is a simply written, practical guide to anyone wanting to turn what might be just a vague idea into a business of some sort. It even starts from the premise that you might not think you have any ideas at all and then helps you to discover that, actually, you probably do. The theme throughout is one of encouragement and positivity and it shies away from the jargon-heavy style of many management manuals.

The first part deals with all of the things that you need to consider before laying the groundwork, including guidance on how to find your idea and trust that it might work. The second part deals with the initial stages of 'starting, dreaming, staying free and learning', before moving on to planning the future for your idea.

The book is written in easily digested sections and through-out you are reminded that hard work and perseverance will pay off. The authors are amiable guides taking you through the process of generating ideas, providing techniques to change your behaviour as you go.

There is a strong emphasis on rejecting procrastination in favour of action and making small, concrete steps each day to achieve your goal. Amor's attitude is that anything can become possible if you take appropriate action. It is quite literally a step-by-step guide taking you from getting your idea down on paper and developing it into an actionable proposition, to making your first tentative steps into the world by testing a 'version zero' of your idea. The emphasis throughout is on learning by doing. Don't feel you have to have a complete business plan worked out before you launch, just get out there and start doing it and you'll learn as you go.

Between the step-by-step guidance are stories from entrepreneurs who have done just what the authors suggest and who recount their own experiences of the process. This is the ideal book for a timid would-be entrepreneur; it doesn't expect you to be already clued up with a great business idea that is ready to launch or presume you are already in a high-flying job. Instead, it encourages anyone and everyone to discover the hidden entrepreneur inside themselves.

THE SPEED READ

The Idea In You

Everyone has a brilliant idea inside them. So stop procrastinating – do it now! Start right away, and learn as you go. You learn things by doing them. Try something every day that you wouldn't normally do – it will give you confidence.

Break in Case of Emergency

Jessica Winter, 2016

*B*reak in Case of Emergency is a novel rather than a business book, but the workplace trials that the main character Jen goes through will seem very relevant and funny to anyone who has ever sat in a meeting, listening to 'business speak', where those in charge stroke their egos and are full of a sense of their own importance yet where nothing concrete is ever said or done and you are nonetheless supposed to leave with an understanding of the tasks you are supposed to fulfil.

Jen has recently found a job at a feminist non-profit organisation run by celebrity philanthropist Leora Infinitas. Called the LiFt foundation, the organisation is meant to be about empowering women around the world. Despite her communications role, very little actual communication takes place. There are pointless meetings in which the staff spend all their time devising acronyms for 'good cause' programmes that are barely explained and understood less. This branding of social causes is set against the backdrop of Leora and her chief co-worker Karina constantly stressing how much they care, which always carries the subtext, 'See what a good person I am.' Karina, who is Jen's boss, is an expert in passive-aggressive behaviour and constantly feeds her acidic 'positive feedback' through whitened teeth while swanning around appearing to be very busy while actually doing very little.

As Jen tries in earnest to pin down what her role is, she is met with generalised answers about the problems faced by women in the developing world and told what an important member of the team she is and how many causes the organisation wants to support. If she asks about achieving something concrete, Jen is told that the organisation doesn't want to 'limit itself' and so the meandering discussion continues. The staff spend their time feeding Leora's ego with the only antidote being Jen's colleague Daisy who perceives the bullshit around her and is able to separate herself from it and support the eager-to-please Jen.

Outside this toxic workplace environment, Jen herself is struggling to conceive a child and is visiting a fertility clinic several mornings a week. It is clear that the organisation's 'empowering women' stance does not apply to those who actually work for them. Karina continuously asks intrusive questions on the assumption that 'sharing is good' and even after Jen has miscarried and is recuperating at home, phones her to tell her to come to a meeting because she is 'appreciated' and 'needed' while showing no concern for Jen herself.

Karina subsequently takes Jen on a business trip to Belize on the excuse that they need to get someone on board to help with financing. It turns out to be really just a freebie for Karina and a way for her to spend time with Travis Paddock, another fundraiser who eventually has to step down for having tax issues. Karina does absolutely no work on this trip (which involves staying at an expensive spa), while Jen does everything to try to secure funding from serial waster and self-involved playboy Bazz Angler.

The core of the comedy throughout is the miscommunication between Jen and Karina. The meaningless language employed by many bosses is key and will resonate with anyone who has been frustrated by a vague line manager. Believing you are actually supposed to understand and to be doing something, you find that the something remains forever undefined because even the boss doesn't really know what they are doing.

THE SPEED READ

Break in Case of Emergency

Non-profit organisations run by celebrity philanthropists are purely a vehicle for the celebrity's own ego. Bosses who don't know what they're doing still expect you to be doing something and will firmly believe that they have told you what to do. Image and branding are more important than actions. It is easy to feel for the plight of women you've never met, but harder to respond with the same sympathy to someone standing right in front of you. And, finally, never take on a job where your role is ill-defined.

Pre-suasion

A Revolutionary Way to Influence and Persuade

Dr Robert Cialdini, 2016

A re you sitting comfortably? Then I'll begin . . . Can I get you a warm drink, something to eat . . . ? Do you like me more now . . . ? People like us enjoy a good cup of coffee, don't we . . . ? See, we're quite alike, aren't we? I think you'll like what I like . . .

Dr Cialdini is a social psychologist who wrote the hugely successful 1984 book *Influence*, which cited six ways in which to persuade people to agree with your message (in his list of jargon: reciprocation, liking, social proof, authority, scarcity and consistency). *Influence* is well worth a read for anyone wanting to understand the ways that consumers and customers are manipulated by sales techniques, whether they want to employ such methods themselves or become immune to them. In *Pre-suasion*, Cialdini expands on the same subject to identify a pre-sales moment, a window of time when there are optimum conditions to deliver your message and for it to be favourably received.

The two main aspects of this moment are based on timing and geographical influence. He claims that you need to set up an environment in which to get the best possible outcome and offers the slightly bizarre example of giving someone a warm drink to hold if you want them to feel warm towards you. You are supposed to be setting the scene by creating favourable conditions seemingly unrelated to the message you are trying to get across. His notion of geographical context is similar to the ways in which advertisers use certain slots in and between programmes they think their customer base will probably watch. Apart from the obvious point of making sure that advertising reaches the right demographic, they hope to tap into the good mood of the consumer who is watching the show. Cialdini calls this 'unity' and argues that this is important in getting the best outcome. His point is that rather than getting your customer to feel good about himself and therefore to feel kindly disposed towards you, you should get him or her to feel a sense of unity, to create a bond before you impart your message which will then be much more likely to be favourably received.

Cialdini has been criticised for the fact that, in spite of saying such techniques should only be used ethically, much of the book advocates diverting attention to where you want to divert it. A magician cleverly focuses your attention elsewhere to astound you with a result you didn't see coming. For Cialdini, this artful sleight of hand leads to successful 'pre-suasion' conditions and gets your target audience in the palm of your hand.

How is this done? Well, you're not changing someone's mind so much as their state of mind. You're trying to get them into the place where you want them to be before sending out your message. This can include choosing a specific time and place to meet or drawing them closer to you by talking about completely unrelated matters to establish some common ground and getting them to engage with you.

Context is a crucial factor here. Cialdini cites studies where seemingly innocuous details influence the outcome of people's choices. He uses the example of two web pages selling the same product, one with a background of coins, the other with clouds. People using the coin background site became more aware of money and chose the cheapest option whereas people using the cloud background site chose quality because the overall message was comfort.

The message is to set the scene and to be creative in where you want the attention of your audience to be *before* you deliver your message. Your target audience is now in a favourable place to receive whatever wisdom you want to impart. This is how you 'pre-suade' them before you try to sell them anything. Putting your audience in a certain frame of mind has been a skill used by confidence tricksters the world over for decades and, in the end, this book merely tells you how best to do it.

THE SPEED READ

Pre-suasion

Timing is everything – there is an optimum window of opportunity to best send out your message. Create that 'key moment' by paying attention to context. Don't try to change someone's mind – change their state of mind. Create a sense of 'unity' between yourself and your audience before you begin. Learn how to divert their attention to the place you want it to be before you give out your message. If your message is of weighty importance, give your audience a heavy breezeblock to hold – they'll get the gravity of the situation. And if all else fails, steal their wallet while pointing out how beautiful the trees are today and gazing out of the window.

Feminist Fight Club

An Office Survival Manual (for a Sexist Workplace)*
*Book is 21 Per Cent More Expensive for Men
Jessica Bennett, 2016

This is an illustrated, entertaining, humorous guide to surviving in the workplace. It's a guide to everyday sexism, dealing with everything from the overt – bordering on harassment – to the more subtle ways men treat women they work with that can undermine their progress.

Bennett draws on experiences and discussions from her very own Feminist Fight Club, a group of women who got together socially to compare notes and share tips about their experiences. Although lacking a wider discussion about how society's structures are often to blame for women failing to get top jobs, Bennett does briefly touch on the historical view of sexism – looking at when it was once acceptable for a man to be openly sexist (including inappropriate touching, language and attitude) – and how we got from there to the society we now live in where some men think that the feminist wars have been fought because women have good professional jobs and there is transparent equality. But, as Bennett points out, attitudes towards women, from stereotyping them into given roles (mother, daughter, wife), to other ways that men behave around women on an everyday basis, show that the workplace is still far from gender-neutral.

Bennett outlines the contradictions that are often at play in the workplace. Being called 'ambitious' is OK if you're a man but means you're domineering and bossy if you're a woman. Women have to be nice, but not too nice or they're seen as a pushover; be confident but not too confident or they're cocky; and caring but not maternal (or, heaven forbid, an actual mother) or they're seen as being not committed to the job. Here, Bennett points out some of the flaws in the attitudes of male colleagues towards their female counterparts and in this respect the book makes some reasonable points.

With her focus on individual strategies for dealing with workplace problems, Bennett then groups men into satirical profiles based on their behaviours. There's the 'Manterrupter' who talks over women in meetings, the 'Menstruhater' who assumes women are hormonal when they are being assertive and sticking to their guns, and the 'Lacthaters' who presume mothers are not committed to the job without judging fathers in the same way. The 'Bropriator' steals your ideas and presents them as their own. Then there is the 'Dismisser' (patronising), the 'Himitator' (arrogant and full of himself) and the 'Stenographucker', who expects women to cover the secretarial and administrative jobs regardless of their role. Of course, men who fit these labels certainly exist but it's questionable whether parodying men is the way to end the stereotyping of women. Bennett believes that confronting such stereotypes is key but fighting fire with fire in this way rarely turns out well because it means that no one ends up actually listening.

Bennett's solutions rely on yet more jargon. There's a section of the book called 'The Fight Moves', advising for instance that when encountering a Manterrupter you should keep talking, keep your pauses short and keep up your momentum. Similarly, when faced with a Bropriator, thank them publicly for picking up on your idea. 'Put the Phucker in His Place', 'Underpromise, Overdeliver', 'Throw to a bro' . . . the terminology continues.

She also uses the term 'Clitoral Mass' (avoiding female marginalisation). The message is that you need to increase the number of women in the room to outmanoeuvre the men. She doesn't fully explain if – or even how – this is practically possible. Bennett refers to women hiring other women as 'Vagaffirmative Action', on the basis that upping the numbers of women in the workplace increases the possibility of more women in powerful roles.

There are three fundamental messages here. Firstly, change the system (accompanied by little in the way of a practical guide); secondly, be able to fight for yourself; and, thirdly, find a girl-gang to support you (your own Feminist Fight Club). Also, avoid being too feminine and carry yourself with the confidence of an unassuming white man. Bennett is most effective when she gives basic advice on how to 'know your enemy' and 'know yourself'. She is here recognising the self-imposed constraints of many women through social conditioning. She says readers should learn to recognise when a male colleague is behaving in a frustrating way, examine their own reactions and think about how they could be perceived. This is where the most useful self-help material in the book comes from.

The book has inevitably come under criticism for its white, privileged viewpoint: Bennett refers to her own Feminist Fight Club members as being part of that group with their professional jobs. The book doesn't really take into account the effect of low-paid menial jobs, race, background or poverty and, while it is amusing, it can be repetitive in its use of jargon. It could equally be criticised for being lightweight. Yes, there are socially conditioned views that men take towards women in the workplace and this needs action but treating it as a joke or a game will not change things. Heavily illustrated, Bennett's work doesn't actually have a huge amount to say and what is said mostly comes in the form of soundbites and witty phrasing. It is best seen as a humorous way of surviving the office day as an individual rather than a real manual for positive change.

THE SPEED READ

Feminist Fight Club

Sexism in the workplace has gone undercover and is now subtle rather than overt – be aware of when it is happening. Men at work can be divided into several stereotypes and there are ways to subtly confront them to stop these behaviours. Know your enemy – recognise the behaviour that you find frustrating. Know yourself – be aware of your own assumptions with regard to your abilities and recognise how your reactions may be perpetuating the problem. Find a female support group for dealing with your problems in the workplace. If you're a woman, hire other women to increase numbers.

Elon Musk

Tesla, SpaceX and the Quest for a
Fantastic Future

Ashlee Vance, 2015

Elon Musk is often described as a real-life Tony Stark (the business magnate in *Iron Man* – Musk even had a cameo role in the second movie in the franchise). Even without the hyperbole, he is a pretty extraordinary individual. One of the world's richest business people, in the first instance because of his creation of Zip2, a software company, and because of his subsequent investment in PayPal, from which he eventually emerged with a huge payment, he has gone on to attempt to turn some seemingly improbable dreams into reality.

He founded SpaceX in 2002 to reduce the cost of space travel and set up a human colony on Mars within the next few decades. His longer-term goal is to facilitate human colonisation of the universe to preserve the existence of the species (threatened not only by the sustainability of life on Earth, but by the eventual expansion of the sun and our planet's destruction). The original aim was to land a miniature greenhouse on Mars to test the viability of growing vegetation in Martian soil. The company has achieved numerous firsts in terms of the types of rockets it has been able to launch and land and Musk continues to aim to send humans to space within ten to twenty years.

Musk became CEO and product architect of Tesla Motors, founded in 2003, after being one of the major early investors. The company has become one of the few successful new start-ups of recent decades in the automobile industry and has made significant progress in reducing the cost of electric vehicles and improving their performance and efficiency.

He is also the largest shareholder in SolarCity, a company founded by two of his cousins, which aims to expand hugely on the use of solar energy. And he is working on Hyperloop, an extraordinary plan to create a new transport system that propels vehicles through a near-vacuum tube at high speeds. In these last three enterprises, Musk's energy and investment have been devoted to the goal of reducing our reliance on renewable energy and combating global warming.

Ashlee Vance's book on Musk tells the whole story of his career, from his difficult childhood in South Africa, through early money-raising activities in Canada, and to his series of remarkable business adventures. Musk doesn't always come across as easy or nice – he can be brutal with both business partners and employees (for instance, according to the book, he effectively sacked his loyal assistant of twelve years after she asked for a pay rise). Like Steve Jobs and other visionary business people, he is clearly extremely driven and egotistical and somewhat blind to his own faults. Vance recognises all of these flaws, but still clearly admires Musk immensely and the book comes to life when he eulogises his achievements at SpaceX and elsewhere.

While more recent titles than this have been reviewed in this book, it seems appropriate to end with a title about Musk because he embodies the idea that business needn't just be about making money. Of course, there are worries about the way in which the future of space travel and the fight against global warming rely so heavily on private companies that are ultimately reliant on the profit factor. But one can still be struck by the fact that Musk has become determined to do what he can to change that future for the better.

Not all of us are lucky enough to have the means or the ability to achieve anything like him. However, he can still be seen as an inspiration to see business as a way of helping to build the future – in how we choose to treat one another as employees and employers, what products we create and how sustainable our activities are, or just in the environment we create for our colleagues and customers in the here and now.

THE SPEED READ

Elon Musk

A recent biography of the extraordinary entrepreneur who is attempting to fight global warming, create better transport options, bring down the costs of space travel and even build a human colony on Mars. Vance's biography is honest about Musk's faults as well as his virtues and we can observe what Musk is doing. We can think hard about what the businesses we build or work for are doing to create a better future.

Bibliography – A Brief Guide to Business Classics

Adams, Scott, *The Dilbert Principle* (1996), Boxtree, London, 2000

Allen, David, *Getting Things Done* (2001), Piatkus, London, 2015

Amor, Martin and Pellew, Alex, *The Idea in You* (2015), Portfolio, London, 2016

Babcock, Linda and Laschever, Sara, *Ask For It* (2008), Bantam, London, 2009

Bakan, Joel, *The Corporation* (2003), Constable & Robinson, London, 2005

Bartiromo, Maria with Whitney, Catherine, *The 10 Laws of Enduring Success* (2010), Crown Business, New York, 2011

Bennett, Jessica, *Feminist Fight Club* (2016), Portfolio, London, 2016

Blanchard, Ken and Johnson, Spencer, *The One Minute Manager* (1982), Jossey Bass, California, 1996

Bogle, John, *Common Sense on Mutual Funds* (1999), John Wiley, New Jersey, 2010

Buffett, Warren, *The Essays of Warren Buffett* (1998), Carolina Academic Press, North Carolina, 2015

Burrough, Bryan and Helyar, John, *Barbarians at the Gate* (1989), Arrow, London, 2010

Carnegie, Dale, *How to Win Friends and Influence People* (1936), Vermillion, London, 2006

Christensen, Clayton M., *The Innovator's Dilemma* (1997), Harvard Business Review, Massachusetts, 2016

Cialdini, Dr Robert, *Pre-suasion* (2016), Random House Business, London, 2016

Collins, Jim, *Good to Great* (2001), Random House Business, London, 2001

Coupland, Douglas, *Microserfs* (1995), HarperPerennial, New York, 2004

Covey, Stephen, *7 Habits of Highly Effective People* (1989), Simon and Schuster, London, 2004

Drucker, Peter, *The Effective Executive* (1967), Routledge, Oxford, 2007

Duhigg, Charles, *The Power of Habit* (2012), William Heinemann, London, 2012

Evans, Gail, *Play Like a Man, Win Like a Woman* (2000), Broadway, New York, 2001

Ferrazzi, Keith, *Never Eat Alone* (2005), Portfolio, New York, 2014

Ferriss, Timothy, *The 4-Hour Workweek* (2007), Vermillion, London, 2007

Fisher, Roger and Ury, William, *Getting to Yes* (1981), Random House Business, London, 2012

Fox, Jeffrey J., *How to Become a Rainmaker* (2000), Vermillion, London, 2013

Frankel, Lois P., *Nice Girls Don't Get the Corner Office* (2004), Business Plus, New York, 2014

George, Bill, with Sims, Peter, *True North* (2007), Jossey-Bass, California, 2007

Gerber, Michael E., *The E-Myth Revisited* (1995), HarperCollins, New York, 2001

Gladwell, Malcolm, *The Tipping Point* (2000), Abacus, London, 2002

Godin, Seth, *Purple Cow* (2003), Penguin, London, 2005

Goldsmith, Marshall, *What Got You Here Won't Get You There* (2008), Profile, London, 2008

Goleman, Daniel, *Emotional Intelligence* (1995), Bloomsbury, London, 1995

Graham, Benjamin, *The Intelligent Investor* (1949), HarperBusiness, New York, 2003

Greene, Robert, *The 48 Laws of Power* (1998), Profile, London, 2000

Hashemi, Sahar and Bobby, *Anyone Can Do It* (2002), Capstone, Oxford, 2002

Hill, Napoleon, *Think and Grow Rich* (1937), Wilder Publications, Virginia, 2007

Isaacson, Walter, *Steve Jobs* (2011), Abacus, London, 2015

Johnson, Spencer, *Who Moved My Cheese?* (1998), Vermillion, London, 1999

Kahneman, Daniel, *Thinking Fast and Slow* (2011), Penguin, London, 2011

Karsan, Rudy and Kruse, Kevin, *We* (2011), John Wiley & Sons, New Jersey, 2011

Klaff, Oren, *Pitch Anything* (2011), McGraw-Hill Education, New York, 2011

Laurence J. Peter, *The Peter Principle* (1969), Souvenir Press, London, 1994

Levinson, Jay Conrad, *Guerrilla Marketing* (1984), Piatkus, London, 2007

Lewis, Michael, *The Big Short* (2010), W.W. Norton, New York, 2010

Lowenstein, Roger, *When Genius Failed* (2000), Fourth Estate, London, 2002

Machiavelli, Niccolò, *The Prince* (1532), Vintage Classics, London, 2008

Mackay, Charles, *Extraordinary Popular Delusions and the Madness of Crowds* (1841), Wordsworth Editions, Hertfordshire, 1995

MacLeod, Hugh, *Ignore Everybody* (2009), Portfolio, London, 2009

Malmsten, Ernst, *Boo Hoo* (2001), Random House Business, London, 2002

McLean, Bethany and Elkind, Peter, *The Smartest Guys in the Room* (2003), Portfolio, New York, 2003

Newport, Cal, *So Good They Can't Ignore You* (2012), Piatkus, London, 2016

Parkinson, C. Northcote, *Parkinson's Law or The Pursuit of Progress* (1958), Infinite Ideas, Oxford, 2011

Patterson, Kerry; Grenny, Joseph; McMillan, Ron; Switzler, Al, *Crucial Conversations* (2002), McGraw-Hill Education, New York, 2011

Pink, Daniel H., *Drive* (2009), Canongate, London, 2011

Ries, Eric, *The Lean Startup* (2011), Portfolio Penguin, London, 2011

Roddick, Anita, *Business as Unusual* (2000), Thorsons, London, 2000

Sandberg, Sheryl, *Lean In* (2013), WH Allen, London, 2013

Schumacher, E. F., *Small is Beautiful* (1973), Abacus, London, 1988

Sinek, Simon, *Start With Why* (2009), Portfolio, London, 2009

Smith, Adam, *The Wealth of Nations* (1776), Wordsworth Editions, Hertforshire, 2012

Taleb, Nassim Nicholas, *The Black Swan* (2007), Random House, New York, 2007

Taylor, Frederick Winslow, *The Principles of Scientific Management* (1911), Martino Fine Books, Connecticut, 2014

Tett, Gillian, *Fool's Gold* (2009), Abacus, London, 2010

Traditional, *The I Ching*, Penguin Books, London, 2010

Trump, Donald and Schwartz, Tony, *The Art of the Deal* (1987), Arrow, London, 2016

Tzu, Sun, *The Art of War* (c. 500 BCE), Capstone, Oxford, 2010

Vance, Ashlee, *Elon Musk* (2016), Virgin, London, 2016

Waterman Jr, Robert H. and Peters, Tom, *In Search of Excellence* (1982), Profile, London, 2015

Watt, James, *Business for Punks* (2015), Portfolio, London, 2016

Weinzimmer, Laurence G. and McConoughey, Jim, *The Wisdom of Failure* (2012), Jossey-Bass, California, 2013

Winter, Jessica, *Break in Case of Emergency* (2016), The Borough Press, London, 2016

Index